I0479556

Invisible & Deviant Mothers:

Childbirth in Visual Culture

1

Rachel Bride Ashton

An imprint of Boom Publications Ltd

272 Bath Street
Glasgow SCOTLAND
G2 4JR

Boom Graduates and the logo are trademarks of Boom Publications Ltd.

Boom Publications Ltd is a more-than-profit company, dedicating over half
our profits to university scholarships for underprivileged students worldwide.
In order to offset our carbon footprint, we also pledge to plant a tree for each
graduation book commissioned.

Invisible & Deviant Mothers: Childbirth in Visual Culture
was first published in Great Britain in 2023.

Typeset by Helen at Boom Graduates.
Printed and bound in the UK.

To find out more about our authors and books visit www.boomgraduates.com
and sign up for our newsletters.

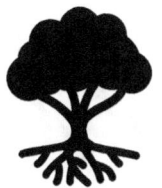

We plant a tree for every
Boom Graduate book commissioned, and
thereafter plant a tree for every 10 books sold.

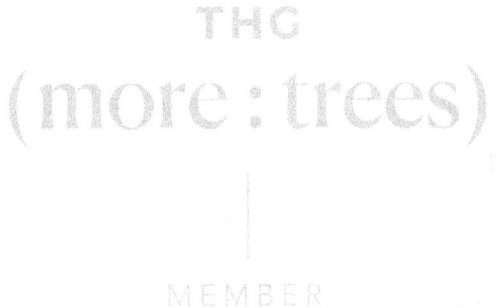

Watch our forest grow at
https://moretrees.eco/forest/BoomPublicationsLtd/

Rachel Bride Ashton

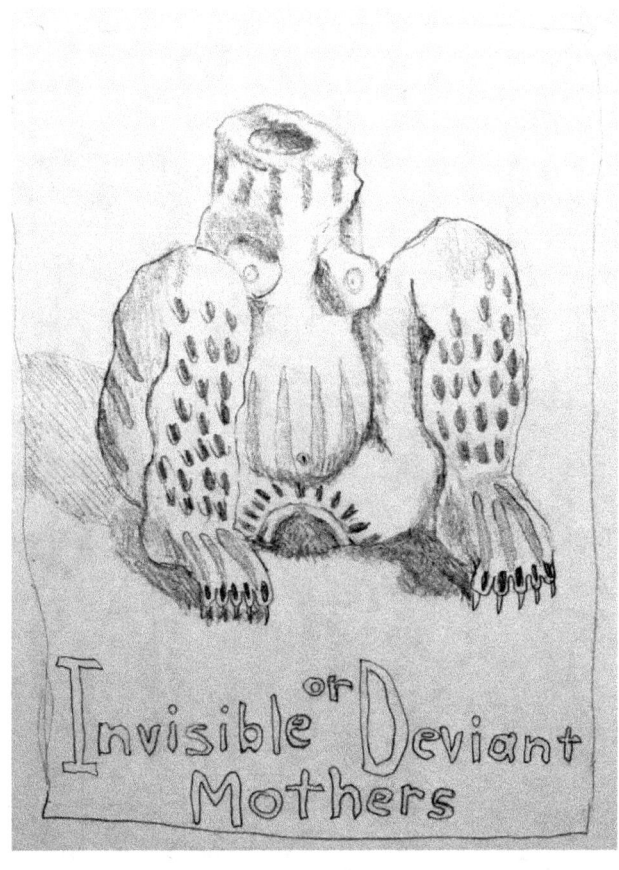

Rachel Bride Ashton

Invisible & Deviant Mothers: Childbirth in Visual Culture

Rachel Bride Ashton

With grateful thanks to the following, for their kind permission to use their images within this book:

Birth Rites Collection

Helen Knowles

Jessica Moore (Jessica Clements)

Jonathan Waller

Rachel Bride Ashton

Contents

Author biography

Rachel Bride Ashton is a Scottish multi-disciplinary artist, researcher and mother whose work advocates for choice in childbirth, challenging our cultural de-animalisation and the institution-controlled birth portrayals dominant in our onscreen culture. Her multi-media installation work celebrates the 90% non-human part of us, our microbiome, formed through undisturbed physiological birth. She became a mother in 1997 and both her babies were delivered at home. She earned her living as a self-taught painter for twenty years while home educating her children and returned to education in 2019. She is the recipient of the Freelands Painting Prize 2022 and won the Dundee Contemporary Arts (DCA) Award, Generator Projects Prize and the James Guthrie Orchar Prize for her first-class undergraduate degree show installation at Duncan of Jordanstone College of Art and Design in 2022.

Abstract

Institution-controlled births have predominated in our fictional on-screen culture for decades. When compared with less frequent home birth narratives, two dominant stereotypes emerge. People giving birth within the medical system tend to be portrayed as good, compliant but invisible, usually passive and not in control, as seen in examples like *E.R.* (1994-2009), *Greys Anatomy* (2017-2020), *Knocked Up* (2007), *Friends* (1994-2004), *Offspring* (2010-2017), *What to Expect When You're Expecting* (2012) *and Sex Education* (2022). Those birthing outside of the hospital, and their attendant midwives are represented as active and visible but deviant and often ridiculous, for example *Grace and Frankie* (2018), *The Gilmore Girls* (2000-2007) and *The Back Up Plan* (2010). More recently *Pieces of a Woman* (2020) challenges the dominant home birth fiasco by exploring a more woman empowered narrative, but ultimately the (deviant) mother is punished by her baby's death, exacerbating deeply ingrained medical hegemony.

Reality television shows, *OBEM* (2010-2018) and *Newborn Russia* (2014), inadvertently expose deep rooted misogyny and obstetric violence at the heart of the medical model of birth. This book argues that globally, on-screen culture could be seen as systemic medical propaganda which turns birth into a process where mothers are secondary to the baby-product. *The Birth Reborn* (2013-2018) documentaries tackle these issues but are alone in highlighting the violence and racial inequalities in maternal care the world over. My method of research combines critical literature with my multi-disciplinary art practice. I embody and represent female tropes and helpful bacteria and reveal the 'deviant woman' as 'maternal holobiont' in complex installations. These portray powerful and active depictions of women-centered birth comparable to recent documentation by femicentric organisations like *Restore Midwifery* (2022), which are beginning to appear on social media. I argue that these could set the precedent for new ways of portraying birth in cinema and television.

Rachel Bride Ashton

Introduction

What do I mean by invisible and deviant mothers? We are used to being surrounded by representations of the mother in our visual world, but what purpose do these images serve? What are the social assumptions that frame these representations? I am particularly interested in how our culture presents the mother in childbirth and whether these presentations can always be categorised as either invisible or deviant.

When I say invisible mothers, I mean that we do not see them. I mean that pregnant women are lost within the institution and have no voice or personal agency. Their births are technocratically and medically controlled.

When I say deviant mothers, I mean those who are seen to be rejecting the Western medical model of childbirth and who demand control over their body and birthing experience.

I propose that institution-controlled births predominate in our visual culture and that this divides women into two dominant stereotypes: the characterisation of women either within the medical system, as good but invisible, or outside of it, as deviant, can be seen as a kind of systemic propaganda.

It could be alleged that cultural publicity turns birth into a process where nothing else matters except the product; the mothers are disposable. This view and the interchange between real world birth and birth in our visual culture has been argued about for decades by feminist scholars, midwives, sociologists and natural birth activists (Kitzinger, Gaskin, Davis-Floyd) and may seem to be an extreme and tired argument, but I believe it is as relevant as ever today.

Considering these tropes of invisible and deviant mothers, I will now examine the examples of childbirth in art and visual culture, under the following more general categories. In chapter one I will consider the mechanising and desexualising of birth and pain, in which I look at the visibility of mothers under capitalism. In chapter two I will examine birth through the lens of perceived obstetric sexual abuse and violence. In chapter three I will analyse the portrayal of home birth as deviance. Finally, in chapter four, I will address the sexuality of birth from the point of view of the person experiencing it and of birth image censorship.

Chapter One:

The Mechanising
and Desexualising of Birth

John Berger in his hugely influential TV series and book, *Ways of Seeing*, states that 'publicity is the life of this culture' (1972). If this is the case, then are we only being shown birth through a capitalist lens. Furthermore, if capitalism continues to exist by forcing us to narrow our interests as far as is possible, then our cultural representations of birth are 'imposing a false standard of what is and is not desirable' (Berger, 1972).

The invisible mother, pregnancy and birth representations.

If the mother is not entirely absent from our culture, she is often, in some way, represented as less visible (fig. 1). The invisible mother is often presented as the good mother.

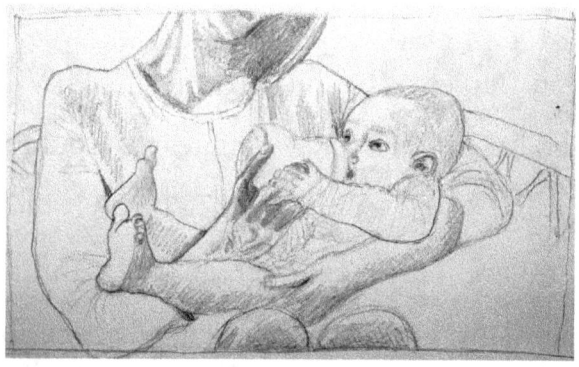

Fig. 1: Rachel Bride Ashton - Pencil drawing impression of *Aptamil* Advert for Follow on Milk (2020).[1]

---

[1] Original available at:
https://m.youtube.com/watch?v=mwtbYhlcdhs.

We are all familiar with this presentation, from the Virgin Mary and child representations in Western painting traditions to the ever-patient, selfless, sugary portrayals of mothers smiling fondly at their children in magazine and TV adverts today. Because of the ingrained traditional Christian connection between sin and sex, the problem with any mother representation is that she is visual evidence of sexual activity and therefore, before the 1960s, unless the image was first desexualised, it was considered taboo (Figes, 2020).

The desexualising and sexualising of mothers in our visual culture could be illustrated by several other time-honoured tropes and dichotomies, the Madonna and Whore, submission and resistance, cyborg and Goddess, and human and animal. When applied to birth narratives it is often a gendered dichotomy between midwifery and medicine. (Allemang in Burton, 2015 p100).

E. Ann Kaplan in 1992, relates 'these representations to the unconscious fears in patriarchy regarding women's sexuality and reproductive capacity' and 'articulates two dominant modes of mother representation – the extremes of mother as either sacrificing "angel" or dominating "witch"' (Williams, 1994), and these tropes endure. Images of pregnant woman proliferate in art now, and more recently in media and predominantly fit within Kaplans desexualized 'Angel' category, with exceptions like Demi Moore's famous *Vanity Fair* cover shot and its enduring controversy.

Until the 1960s and 70s, images of pregnant women were rare (Figes, 2020). Representations of birthing mothers, however, are far rarer in visual art, and Tereza Stejskalova comments on the lack of representation of 'birthing bodies' by art institutions and proposes that this is not discussed enough in academia (2019). Though birth scenes now proliferate in media culture, in drama, reality TV and film, the birthing mother herself is very often portrayed as passive, peripheral, psychologically absent and her face and personality are often missing altogether from the birthing scene. In fictional scenes of medical emergency, for example, in the popular Nineties American TV series ER and Grey's Anatomy, women are frequently hidden under oxygen masks, behind monitors and screens, obscured by staff, under sheets.

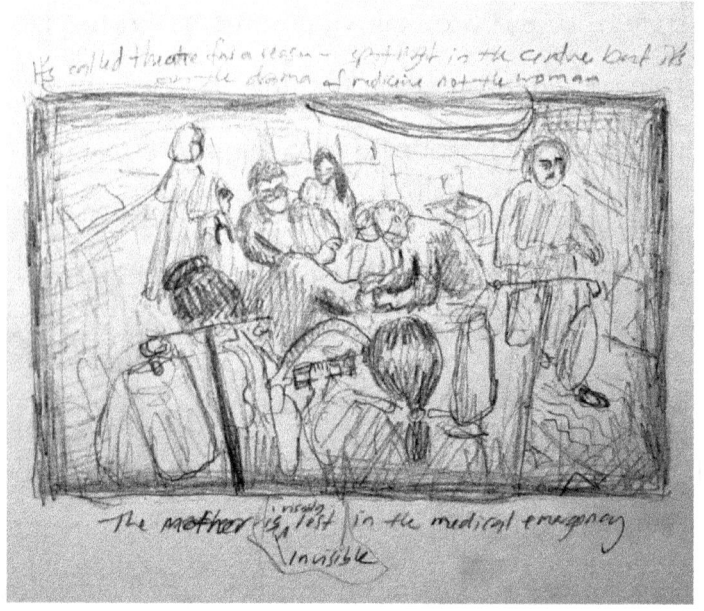

Figure 2 – Rachel Bride Ashton - Pencil drawing impression of ER - *Love's Labor Lost* Season 1 Episode 19 (1995).[2]

The first representational shift of significance that Kaplan identifies for the mother in film is that of

---

[2] Original available at:
https://www.youtube.com/watch?v=qiwvKqxWecw&list=RDCMUCmFOrXia93QJEU2WwbL4irQ&index=2

achieving a most basic human capability: her own subjectivity. Traditionally "an absent presence." The mother's influence in literary fiction and film was almost always presented from the point of view of an "other"' (Williams, 1994). I believe this applies also in representations of women birthing.

Einion argues that 'the key feature of this subject role in representations of birth is that it not only places the woman in a position of having less power than the institution which surrounds her but that she has no voice in this institution (Burton, 2015 p.175).

Social anthropologist, author and natural birth activist Sheila Kitzinger describes birth as a medical event in which the woman is expected to be a good, quiet and compliant patient and points out that 'the word 'patient' itself derives from 'passivity'; a patient is someone to whom something is done' (Kitzinger, 1992 p133-5).

Perfectly compliant patients don't generally make for good comedy unless it's making fun of the good behaviour itself, like the character who is the perfect patient in What to Expect When Your expecting, who gives birth with no sound or fuss (just a little lady-like sneeze). There is plenty of scope for humour within the flighty or capricious mother stereotype, however, which falls within the good mother trope as she's ultimately subjugated. In the film *Knocked Up* the birthing protagonist is portrayed as comedically and prettily neurotic while being compliant enough within the medical system. Sweetly insistent on a natural birth (backed by her male partner) but typically changes her mind and demands the epidural. The young male nurse's demand; 'can you try to keep it down a bit, you'll upset the other mothers,' shows an ironic self-awareness of this expectation of quietness raised by Kitzinger. He is given short shrift by the protagonist, who could be said at this point, to be displaying slightly deviant behaviour. She is brought back in line however by the famously airbrushed 'crowning baby' scene, with neat, pink, bald labia stretched around an unconvincing head which allows a show of the correct amount of disgust and horror by the mother and a young male friend as he bursts into the room. Much humour is derived from his extended traumatised exclamations about the 'wrongness' of what he's seen to his friends in the waiting room. This I believe, like Kaplan, that though representations of mothers are everywhere, they are 'usually seen through an androcentric perspective and/or the male gaze' (Bauer, 2002) and reinforcing this argument is the fact that most of the films and TV series I mention here are directed by men.

The birthing woman as spectacle in the public arena, her body and behaviour as comedy, is a staple of birth scene entertainment. We see again and again this trope of the capricious birthing woman within a comedy narrative arc. For example, the woman (or couple) with the excessively long and well-presented birth plan who wants a natural birth until the pain gets too much, at which point she screams for drugs (either at the first contraction or when it's too late to have any). Another common narrative is that the women's body 'malfunctions' and modern medicine is ready to step in and save the baby with surgery, but the poor deluded woman doesn't understand and thinks her planning will save her; "But I typed it. Its typed, the birth plan, its ready to go, I'm ready to push." Followed soon after by her dreamy/happy pronouncement "I love morphine" when she's in theatre (*What to Expect When You're Expecting*). Other examples of this subduing of the woman's voice and dismissing her wishes is evident in both, *Look Who's Talking* and *Knocked Up*.

During the whole of the Twentieth Century, and up until the Birth Rites Collection began in 2006, which I will talk about in Chapter four, there are only two graphic paintings of birth I could find by notable artists, which stand out and which also strikingly illustrate the invisible mother trope.

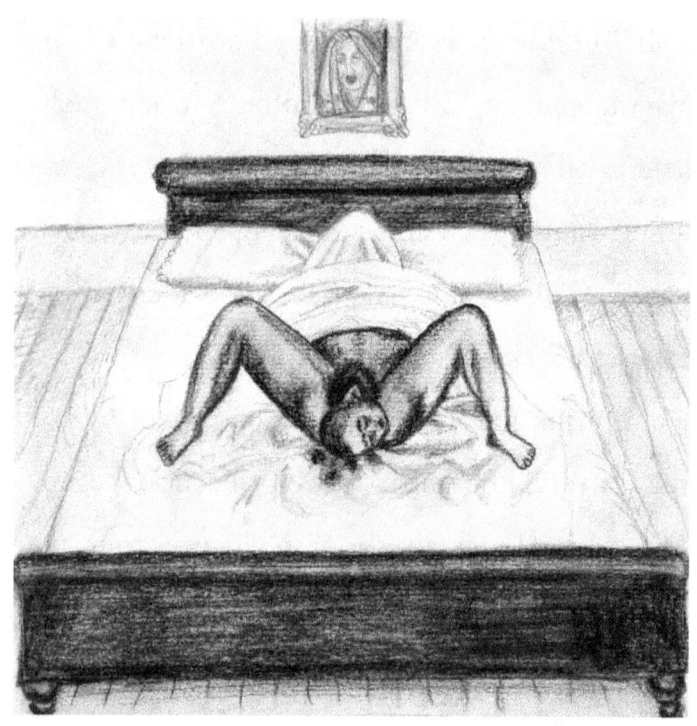

Figure 3 - Rachel Bride Ashton – Charcoal and pencil drawing impression of Frida Kahlo - *My Birth* (1932).[3]

---

[3] Original available at:
https://www.fridakahlo.org/my-birth.jsp

The first is Frida Kahlo's *My Birth* (1932) (fig.3). It is an imagined birth scene, apparently representing Kahlo herself being born. It was painted following a miscarriage and her mothers' death. (Winant, 2016). The birthing mother is on her back on a bed, upper body and face covered by a white sheet. Her legs are wide open, and the baby's head and neck are already out. Although the sheet may have been intended as a death shroud, it also eliminates the mother's identity, dehumanises her, objectifies and mechanises her. She appears discarded and alone. It clearly echoes the grief and trauma in Kahlo's life, but also reads as an uncomfortable symbol of the minimising of women and their mechanised function and disposability within capitalism.

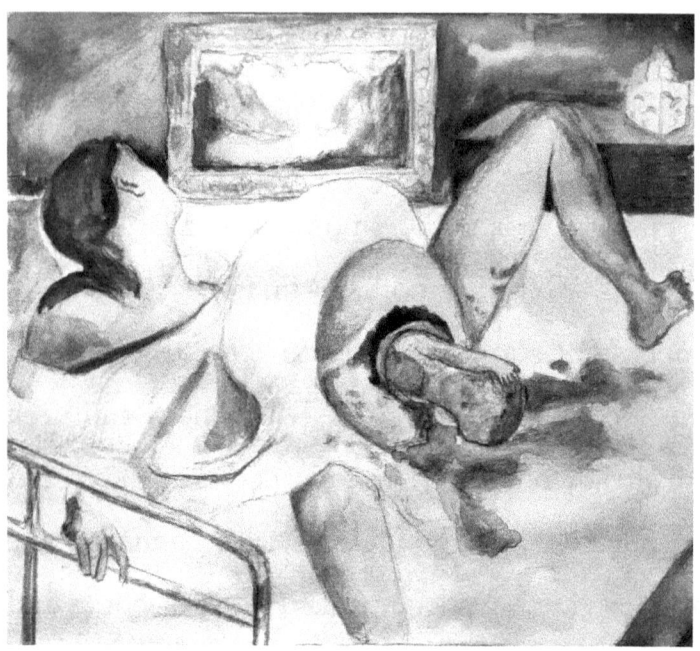

Figure 4 - Rachel Bride Ashton - Watercolour impression of Dana Schutz - *How We Would Give Birth* (2007).[4]

---

[4] Original available at:
https://contemporaryartreview.la/the-art-of-birth/

The second painting is, *The Way We Would Give Birth* by Dana Schutz (fig. 4). Schutz herself admitted that she painted it before she'd experienced childbirth personally and after the event, she would have painted it very differently (Winant, 2016).

The birthing women's face is turned away, looking over her shoulder towards a glowing golden landscape painting on the wall almost behind her. Like the Kahlo painting she is on her back on a bed with white sheets, but in this painting, she is bathed in golden light. Does this mean that Schutz believes that art functions as calming and therapeutic or that we look to nature to escape what is perceived to be the medical horror that is birth? It is not a medical setting however, and she seems to be alone in a homely bedroom though she lies on what appears to be a hospital bed. Her features are not visible at all. In the forefront of the painting, the blood-spattered baby is at a similar stage of exit to that of the Kahlo painting and has barely any discernible features. In fact, it looks more like an oversized early-stage foetus than a new-born. The focus of the painting at first seems to be the visceral emergence of the baby, but on further examination the connection between the woman and the painting on the wall seems more important.

It is another example of the absent mother and seems to me to be a very literal depiction of how we turn away from what we culturally perceive as the trauma and the labour of birth. She is on her back, propped on her elbows, staring over her shoulder towards a painting on the wall behind her and seems passive and completely distracted and disconnected from the process her body is going through. Her upper body is covered with a sheet or possibly a medical gown which may represent the Cartesian divide between mind and body.

In service to the fetus

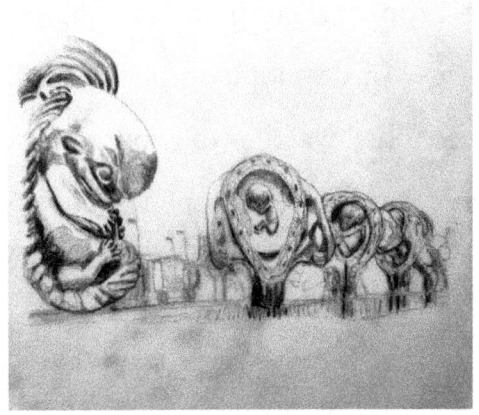

Figure 5 - Rachel Bride Ashton - Pencil drawing impression of Damien Hirst - *The Miraculous Journey* (2013).[5]

---

[5] Original available at:
https://www.theguardian.com/world/2018/nov/19/damien-hirst-delivers-controversy-with-giant-uterus-sculptures-at-qatar-hospital

A more contemporary example however, and a perfect paradigm of the invisible mother, is Damien Hirst's giant sculptures in Qatar (fig.5), which are installed outside a hospital for Women and Children. *The Miraculous Journey* (2013) is a massive series of bronze sculptures showing a fetus at various stages of development, the last of which is an independent, walking newborn. The starkly schematic, scientific, sliced-open wombs minus the mother, bring to mind Rosalind Pollack Petchesky's assessment of the earliest photos of a fetus in utero, in popular literature, in her essay, *Fetal Images: The Power of Visual Culture in the Politics of Reproduction* written in 1987: 'In every picture the fetus is solitary, dangling in the air (or its sac) with nothing to connect it to any life-support system but "a clearly defined umbilical cord"'. She claims that these images compound the idea of the autonomous fetus and missing woman. Hirst's work, like Petchesky's fetal images, embodies 'the aura of medical authority' and 'the allure of technology' (1987, p.268). Contrary to what Hannah Clugston, writer for *The Guardian* believes about the sculptures being 'a rare celebration of women's bodies, vividly quashing art's tendency to sanitise birth' (2018), I am of the view that Hirst has carved up the disposable woman. He has cut the mother away and recreated a relic, a massive series of sanitised monuments which epitomise the concept of the baby as product. Very much like as Petchesky described in 1987, the sculptures embody depletion under industrial capitalism, female compliance, and imperial power (p.268). Kitzinger, who believes that a culture's core values are betrayed by their birth and death ceremonies, (2012) and talks of obstetricians enacting ceremonials on high altars [in 1992], reveals Hirst's sculptures as saying nothing new. They suggest cold metal and cutting. Caesarean sections, despite being lifesaving in the appropriate cases, are performed far more frequently than is medically necessary and the rate continues to rise globally (World Health Organisation, 2021). This surgical appropriation of a physiological event is both born out of and reinforces the idea that the fetus is independent of the peripheral and disposable mother. Barbara Katz Rothman describes the fetus as a fetish and a metaphorical spaceman, a homunculus, that leaves the mother as nothing but space (Petchesky, 1987, p.268). In the film *Look Who's Talking* (1989), the writer gives the baby a voice and character while he is still in utero, encouraging, as Chikako Takeshita suggests, pro-life organisations' arguments about 'fetal personhood' and damaging the decade-long arguments for reproductive rights (2017). Petchesky proposes that the fetus is attached by nothing except its umbilical cord to the spaceship, or we could call it the mothership, which brings us to the idea of the mother as machine.

The body as machine

Medicalised or technocratic birth portrayals can be seen in *Look Who's Talking*, *Knocked Up*, *What to Expect When Your Expecting*, *The Women*, *Baby Mama*, *Nine Months*, *Juno* and in TV series like *ER*, *Friends*, *Grey's Anatomy*, *Offspring*, *One Born Every Minute*, *Newborn Russia*, *Midwives*, *Sex Education* – the list goes on. When we picture a woman giving birth, we generally picture her either fully or partially reclined on a hospital bed and wired up to multiple monitoring machines.

Donna Haraway famously said she would rather be a cyborg than a goddess (Karremann, 2004), and despite trying to dispel the technology-nature binary, her statement for me encapsulates the continuing divide in women's attitudes to pain in childbirth and to one another perpetuated in on-screen culture. Those who have delivered under technological control and anaesthesia or by caesarean often feel they are being judged as failures by those who have unmedicated, vaginal deliveries and who wear their achievement like a badge of honour. The cyborg is a perfect analogy for the modern-day desexualized birthing woman. The medical professionals' eyes are not on the woman, but on the screens of the machines which monitor her body (Kitzinger, 1992, p.143). The machine-managed birth model clearly states to the world that a woman's body, like an old car, is in danger of breaking down. (Kitzinger, 1992, p.143). Despite Haraway's efforts to embrace the cyborg as a feminist tool (Karremann, 2004), this medically controlled cyborg narrative has only increased since the Nineties despite evidence that noisy, intrusive medical environments with their harsh lighting and accompanying anxiety have negative effects on normal birth. In addition, monitoring and epidurals carry risks and the potential to halt labour, affect breastfeeding (Newnham et al., 2017) and affect the long-term health of both mother and child (Phillips, 2018). Knowing this, medicine will still blame the mechanical body and look for further technological solutions (Newnham et al, 2017).

The first part of a three-part Netflix documentary, *The Birth Reborn*, which highlights the extremely high caesarean rate in Brazil, makes it clear that this technocratic birth model is a product of capitalism. Doctors are paid more to perform a caesarean (or any intervention), while natural birth makes no money. C-sections can be scheduled to suit the surgeon and are far quicker than supporting a natural labour and birth, which could take up a hospital room and staff time for days. Anthropologist and author, Robbie Davis-Floyd, interviewed in the programme says there is no evidence to support the caesarean rate being so high, in Brazil or worldwide. She says doctors have forgotten how to do vaginal birth and can't even palpate to determine the baby's position anymore, because they have an ultrasound machine to do it for them (2013).

The infamous mid-labour emergency C-section has been the mainstay of many a TV series over the last thirty years and makes for high emotional and comedic drama and entertainment

(*ER*, *Grey's Anatomy*, *Offspring*, and *What to Expect When you're Expecting*.) Is it possible that this 'culture of caesareans' is part of the process of desexualising birth? If we consider that a C-section is the rerouting of a baby's exit into the world from a woman's vagina to her stomach, through a controlled, sterile, technological, surgical procedure, in which she has no sensation in the lower half of her body, it might seem so. The inverse of a cyborg would be a human animal and Western culture views the human female animal as the antithesis of all that a woman should be. In their essay *Refusing Delinquency, Reclaiming Power – Indigenous Woman and Childbirth*, Clair Dion Fletcher and Cheryllee Bourgeois affirm that dehumanising representations of indigenous women are commonplace in historical accounts by settler societies (2015, p.158). They also draw attention to

47

the "Beasts of Burden" narrative, which represents indigenous women's births as 'easy, sexualised, and/or animal-like due to closeness with nature compared to the civilised European women' (2015, p.159). The effect of colonialism on birth in indigenous cultures is a separate area of research however and I am unable to do it justice here.

The popular British reality TV show, *One Born every Minute* (*OBEM*), shows typical narratives of the powerful institution intervening and delivering the baby for the woman in need (Enion, 2015, p.182). In Alys Enion's words, 'here we see the worst kind of gender stereotypes and gender roles played out, without any challenge'. In the very first episode the birthing woman is mocked for the noises she makes by her husband and teenage son and is upsettingly unsupported. The programme's editing produces a narrative which validates "male superiority" and debases the woman, the inferior subject, for her "animal nature" (2015, p.184). The same woman who is teased for the noises she makes, is then teased again by her husband for asking for pain relief when she'd said she wanted a natural birth. In both the U.K. and U.S. versions of the programme, women are shown to be at peace when on pain medication and those who are unmedicated "are shown to be in agony" (Cummins, 2019) and yet the husband's accusation still exposes her request as a failure.

This common trope of a woman unable to bear the pain of childbirth is discussed in Natalie Jolly's *Does Labour mean Work? A Look at the Meaning of Birth in Amish and Non-Amish Society.* Jolly proposes that in America 'the components of normative femininity devalue a woman's ability to endure pain, to work hard, and to prevail in the face of adversity.' She goes on to say that, conversely, these same components are 'emblematic' of the Amish communities' understanding of femininity (2015, p.218).

The noises the woman makes in *OBEM* may make the men in the room uncomfortable precisely because they sound like sex noises. Kitzinger judges that sexuality and female energy in the context of birth are considered dangerous and threatening and are suppressed in a medical setting. 'Birth it is implied, is simply *pain*, and doctors can manage pain' (Kitzinger, 1992). There is no discussion about the fact that for many women, myself included, pain and pain relief are not the right words, and that the enormity of the sensations felt during birth maybe share more with orgasm than pain. The same hormones are in fact released during sexual arousal and childbirth (Chawla,

2016), which I will say more about in chapter four. An epidural to numb the pain of surgical cutting makes sense but numbing the lower half of the body also interferes with instinctive positioning in response to contractions. Epidurals, in other words, not only take away women's control over their bodies, but they stop them from following their more animal instincts, for example squatting and crawling. They also lessen the desire to roar, scream, moan and gasp - noises they might also make during sex.

The predominantly unnecessary practice of cutting a baby from the stomach of a healthy low-risk mother through dangerous surgery is now being shown, by the latest scientific research, to deny a new-born baby the necessary bacteria for a properly working immune system. Natural birth, complete with faecal and vaginal bacteria and labour-activated breast milk bacteria, imbues the new-born with a healthy microbiome designed to provide the child with disease resistance for life (Collen, 2015). With this bacterial symbiosis in mind, Takeshita calls on us to see 'the pregnant body as a *holobiont*, or an integrative symbiotic system…making it more difficult to make claims about an independent fetus or to negate the benefits of natural birth' (2017). These breakthrough findings will of course take a long time to filter into the mainstream consciousness and into onscreen birth narratives, despite awareness in the scientific community for at least the last six years. The routine use of antibiotics before and after a C-section should be of far bigger concern however, as the antibiotic resistance crisis has been recognised as one of the biggest threats to human health since at least 2013 but has been of increasing concern since the early eighties. The only negative reference to a C-section I could find onscreen was a dismissive reference in the Australian TV comedy drama series *Offspring* by the obstetrician, who disregards a woman's reluctance to have a caesarean because she had heard it was more difficult for a mother to bond with a 'Caesar baby'. Post-surgery, women are unable to hold their babies or attempt to breast feed for often hours afterwards, which has shown to cause problems with breastfeeding, bonding, and the mother's mental health (Block, 2007).

Chapter Two

Sexualising Birth
and Obstretric Violence

Stejskalova mentions the 'complete absence' of the crowning baby's head in popular culture (2021) and I would argue that this absence is sexualising the process of birth by censoring it. The soft-focus blurring of the birthing women's pubic areas in *Newborn Russia* (Fig. 7), like Instagram's censoring of the female nipple, judges these body parts, even in their reproductive capacity, too sexual to show. But by blurring out these areas of the body, could this not be considered titillation? I will discuss censorship in more depth in chapter four.

Birthing positions and lack of consent – Newborn Russia

The supine, dorsal or horizontal birthing position, variations of which are - lateral (on the side), semi-recumbent (partially propped up upper-body), lithotomy (feet in stirrups), have only been used in the last two hundred years in Western cultures. There is much pictorial and written evidence that, prior to this, upright postures, including squatting, standing and kneeling were used almost exclusively in most cultures throughout the world. There is much speculation as to why this change in position occurred, but the predominant theory seems to be that it was because of the development of obstetric surgery (Dundes, 1987). Studies have been conducted since, which show that gravity can help in upright positions, labour speeds can increase and that women overwhelmingly prefer being upright (Watkins, 2019), and yet birthing women are still predominantly shown in supine positions in our onscreen culture.

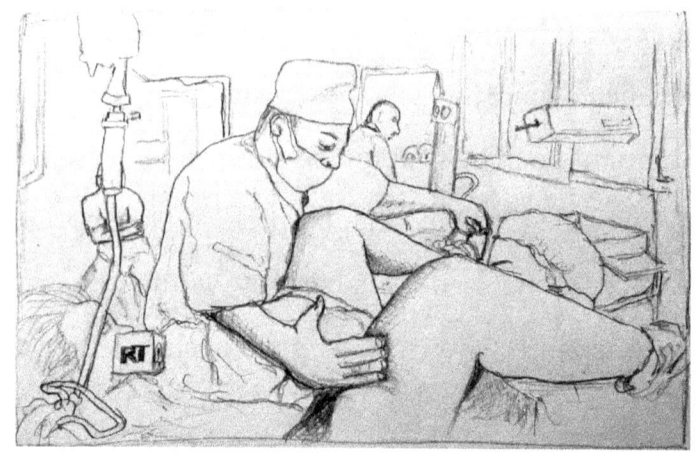

Figure 6 – Rachel Bride Ashton - Pencil drawing impression of Newborn Russia - *firstborn for internet dating soulmates* E23 (2014).[6]

The Russian version of *OBEM*, *Newborn Russia* shows all woman being delivered in the lithotomy position without exception (Fig. 6). If they try to change position they are told not to or are

---

[6] Original available at:
https://www.youtube.com/watch?v=7JcynfS9RBM

physically restrained with subtle violence. In episode twenty-three for example, the mother is told repeatedly not to scream and as she raises her head during a pushing contraction, the male doctor pinches her nose and uses it to push her head back onto the pillow. She is given confusing instructions, for example being told that she is going to break her baby's neck while being shouted at to push ('Firstborn for Internet Dating Soulmates', 2014). The harsh way in which the women are controlled, reprimanded, belittled, threatened and given orders by the medical staff makes for disturbing viewing (2014).

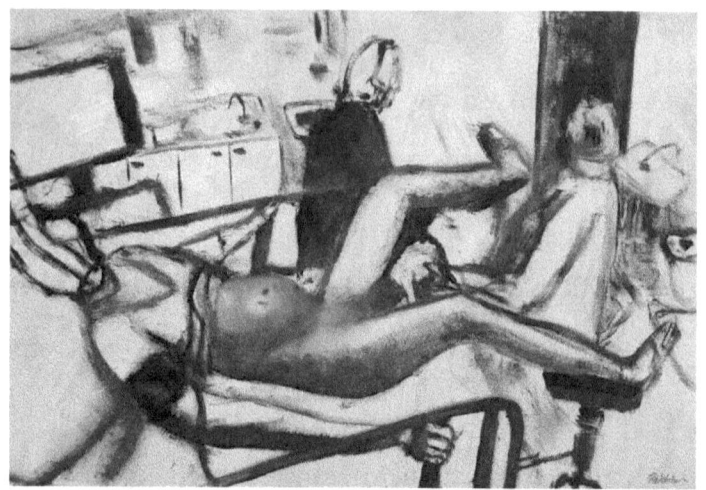

Figure 7 - Rachel Bride Ashton – Oil on board impression of Newborn Russia - Giving birth without an epidural E9 (2014).[7]

The births in both *Newborn Russia* and *OBEM* are managed and filmed with the baby as subject, the woman as object and the hospital staff as heroes.

---

[7] Original available at:
https://www.youtube.com/watch?v=nQoxtHMVZ X8

The women are disempowered physically and psychologically. They thank the medical staff after delivery as if they themselves had no part in the process.

When comparing these hospital birth scenes with YouTube videos of women or their partners filming their own unattended births at home, which I discuss in the last chapter, the difference in agency is extreme.

Shelia Kitzinger believes that for many women, '[birth is] an experience comparable to rape', and evidence is growing to suggest that postnatal depression is in fact, post-traumatic stress disorder (Kitzinger, 2012, Nonacs, 2020).

Einion believes 'it is possible to draw a direct comparison between the narrative structures (textual and visual) that represent women as victims of physical and sexual violence and those that represent woman as "victims" of the birth process' (Einion, 2015, p182). The lithotomy position, also called the gynaecological position, is also of course a woman's orientation in the missionary position. Barbara Bradby writes in *Like a Video: The Sexualisation of Childbirth in Bolivia* (1998) that rural woman who were delivered in hospital in the lithotomy position, lying with their legs spread in front of male doctors, were extremely upset by what they felt to be the sexualization of birth, involving 'manual penetration' of fingers by male doctors, sometimes several in succession (1998). Accordingly, almost every on-screen birth scene involves the ubiquitous vaginal examination, usually accompanied by 'I'm going to examine you now' as statement of intent and not a seeking of consent. Sara Cohen Shabot believes that within a patriarchal framework, sexual violence is not recognized as violence and that because of this, vaginal examinations during birth are not acknowledged as violence by birthing women, nor by obstetrics staff (Shabot, 2020). Yet we know from multiple recent mainstream news coverage that unacceptable numbers of women in the real world suffer reproductive injustice, in the form of physical or verbal abuse and social and racial discrimination, and receive surgical interventions against their will (Bohren, 2019, Kasprzak, 2019, Limb, 2021, Summers, 2021).

Burton however 'does not equate the *experience* of birth with sexual violence' but 'equates the *representation* of birth with the *representation* of sexual violence. Both representations show women in various stages of resistance and submission.' She goes on to cite examples in, among others, *OBEM* and *The Handmaids Tale*, which I am not examining here.

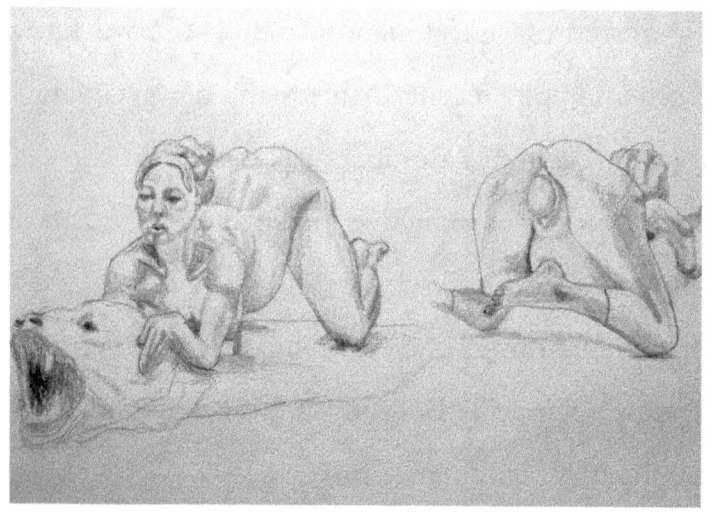

Figure 8 - Rachel Bride Ashton - Pencil drawing impression of Daniel Edwards - Monument to pro-life: The Birth of Sean Preston (2016).[8]

---

[8] Original available at:
http://www.arthistoryarchive.com/arthistory/contemporary/Controversial-Britney-Sculpture.html

Monument to pro-life: The Birth of Sean Preston by Daniel Edwards

I mention Daniel Edwards *Monument to pro-life: The Birth of Sean Preston* (2016), as it is the only portrayal of a woman giving birth on all fours which I could find in the contemporary art world (fig.8). But is this fictional portrayal of pop icon Britney Spears a sexualized representation of birth seen through the 'male gaze' or a celebration of fertility, childbirth, and motherhood as the artist claims? Edwards chose a provocative title but denies holding either a pro-life or a pro-choice stance. Spears opted for an elective caesarean, telling Elle magazine in 2005 that she wanted to avoid the pain of vaginal birth (Jolly, 2015, p.219), but in the sculpture, Edwards has her labouring on her elbows and knees on a bear skin rug. She has virtually no expression and her hands caress the bear's head. Her back is arched

65

in a position more reminiscent of sex than birth, at least within our western cultural understanding of birth. The baby's head is crowning, and she has no pubic hair. Her position is animalistic, hinted at further by the bear's head. It's an interesting work though, because I believe it can be viewed in a number of ways. It could be argued that the sculpture is voyeuristic and certainly the Capla Kesting Gallery printed in their catalogue, emails they had received from men complaining that there were no pictures of the rear view on their website. It is certainly an idealized and romanticized representation. Edwards chose a celebrity who chose not to give birth vaginally to be the subject of a sculpture exemplifying natural birth, celebrating the fact that he saw her to be choosing motherhood over her career. Either he is criticising the objectifying, commodifying, and sexualising celebrity body culture and the sculpture is ironic, or it is a powerful celebration of women's sexuality, rarely seen in connection with birth. Or it is an objectifying, voyeuristic, pro-porn symbol, where the crowning babies head represents an emerging penis. He is reported to have said that he sees Spears as a modern fertility goddess. I may be being generous to Edwards in suggesting that all these elements were considered. Judging by his other art, he could conceivably have been trying to do nothing more than be controversial. But should it be viewed as empowering or objectifying? Spears, whose permission was never asked, was horrified by the sculpture, and felt it was the latter, likening the sculpture to 'some twisted porno' (Bear, 2006). This work has become inadvertently more relevant today, considering Spears' recent legal battle with her father (whom she charged with conservator abuse) for autonomy over her reproductive rights (Savage, 2021).

The very new and current British series *Sex Education* ended its recent series with a disappointingly familiar birth scene. The supposedly forward-thinking, sexually empowered and feminist Jean Millburn was positioned on her back in a hospital bed, restricted as usual by monitors and drips and straining against gravity (Episode 7, 2021). There is a scene where Jean is in the corridor and the male doctor addresses the father of the baby instead of her, which feeds into the invisible woman trope and patriarchal power structure, but in a series which seems to pride itself in tackling racism, sexual abuse, gender, and sexuality, they missed the perfect opportunity to tackle, at the very least, the lithotomy position hegemony

Chapter Three

Home Birth as Deviance

In this chapter, I introduce the deviant mother trope, in the form of the pregnant mother who says no to a medicalised birth and sometimes in the form of the deviants who assist her. Contrary to what Stejskalova writes about cinematic birth being romanticised (2019), I believe that typical on-screen birth narratives behave as cultural publicity which often focus on what can go wrong. These narratives perpetuate fear and anxiety about birth in the real world (Rink, 2012), making moral judgements about homebirth choices and thereby keeping childbirth within the control of the institution. I would agree, however, that medicalised births are sometimes romanticised when juxtaposed with homebirths. In our visual culture, to reject institutional and medical conventions is seen as deviant, subversive, animalistic and extremist and often laughable or dangerous. A recent review in *The Lancet* however, found no difference in risk between giving birth in hospital or at home (Hutton, 2019). A study also found, by examining the influences behind women's decisions to use an epidural in labour, that 'institutional surveillance' increased risk to women by trying to keep them safe, calling this the '*Paradox of the Institution*' (Newnham et al, 2017). For Jessica D. Clements in her thesis, *The Origin of the World – Women's Bodies and Agency in Childbirth* (2009) (and for myself) 'the choice to birth unmedicated at home is profoundly rooted in feminist ideology: the choice is about a woman's inherent power and about claiming one's own body' (Clements, 2009). In addition to the deviant mother tropes, this deviance is sometimes demonstrated in the form of the midwives or doulas who attend homebirths. Elizabeth Allemang in her essay, *Heroes and Villains - Representations of Midwives in Ontario's Late Twentieth Century Midwifery Revival*, outlines three tropes: The counterculture midwife, the feminist midwife, and the aspiring professional (2015). Considering the TV shows which include storylines where women opt for midwife-attended home births, this choice is represented as 'irrational' opines Lauren Elizabeth Rink, who references 'Prime-time shows such as *Gilmore Girls*, *Girlfriends*, and *Dharma & Greg*'. She adds that 'such depictions misrepresent the midwifery model of obstetric care and ultimately affirm the need for the dominant medical model of birth' (Rink, 2012).

Falling into the trap of being nostalgic about the superiority of midwives and childbirth in the past as Allemang thinks many writers and activists are inclined to do (for example, Arms; Baldwin; Davis; Gaskin; Lang) or getting stuck in the nature/science and gendered binaries, only increases the tension between medicine and midwifery (2015 p.100). This tension is evident in the ongoing portrayal of midwives as unsuitable caregivers and stigmatized society rejects, by their association with, or influence over, the deviant mothers and home births they attend. They are shown as comic villains, 'transgressors' and ultimately to be laughed at (Rink, 2012).

Jeff Nall in *Interrogating Social Conceptualizations of Childbirth and Gender, An Ecofeminist Analysis,* surmises that the American film, *The Backup Plan*, is an 'overtly patriarchal moral tale of the pitfalls and buffoonery of disavowing heteronormativity' (2011, p.124). He also postulates that 'the film draws on the homophobic association of lesbianism with dirtiness to mark homebirth as a filthy, feminine-forsaking enterprise' (2011, p.125). I agree with his assessment, and add to this, that the film utilises propaganda to make a hideous and prolonged slapstick joke out of matriarchal support and 'woman empowered' homebirth.

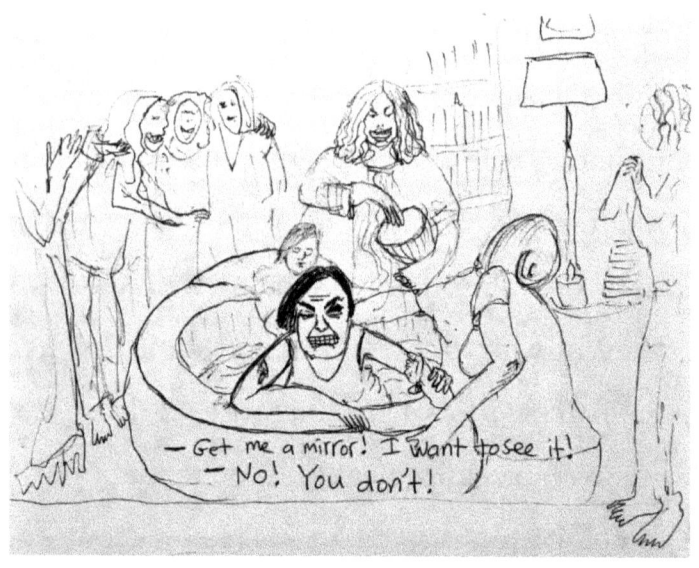

Figure 9 – Rachel Bride Ashton - Pen drawing
impression of The Backup Plan (2010).[9]

The scene is executed using every counterculture
cliché imaginable. Rocking and chanting women,
tattoos, piercings and dreadlocks, a foolish midwife
(Allemang's first trope), singing unintelligible

---

[9] Original available at:
https://www.youtube.com/watch?v=6PYiiJOH6T0

sounds, banging a drum (possibly referencing indigenous birth rituals) and shouting predictable 'hippy' phrases. The animalistic birthing mother, roars aggressively and pulls ugly faces in a birthing pool (fig. 9). She demands a mirror, to see the crowning baby's head and then defecates in the pool, causing the heroine, played by the glamorous and horrified Jenifer Lopez, to faint into the water after she exclaims in disgust at the sight of the birthing mother's pubic hair. The pregnant Lopez, the epitome of patriarchal, normative and desirable femininity, is rescued by her husband from the traumatic experience. Their subsequent conversation validates societal horror of female natural bodily processes, body hair and empowerment and dismisses the deviant woman for her outrageous and subversive choices. *The Backup Plan* ends with a passive and prone Lopez having an idealized, short, heavenly lit, medicalised birth (2010), backing up Stejskalova's theory about the romanticising of onscreen birth (2021). The 'medicalized birth...becomes identified with the "happily ever after" of patriarchal heteronormativity' (Nall, 2011, p.125).

Stejskalova says that seeing birthing bodies 'trigger experiences of abjection, that is, disgust, horror, danger, repulsion' (2021), which is clearly demonstrated in this film. Nall adds to this that the childbirth scenes in both the films *The Backup Plan* and *Knocked Up* suggest a transformation of the vagina from 'an object of sexual desire to an organ of horror and revulsion" and that 'only within patriarchal gender boundaries that systematically marginalize female sexual and reproductive potency would women's birthing agency be met with such fear and bewilderment' (2011, p.131).

The home birth in the purportedly subversive Netflix American sitcom, *Grace and Frankie* (2018) is a hastily planned home waterbirth. The cannabis smoking hippy, Frankie, who is an ex-commune-living, counterculture doula, arrives just in time to deliver her daughter-in-law's baby, with a to-be-mocked, culturally appropriated birth ceremony.

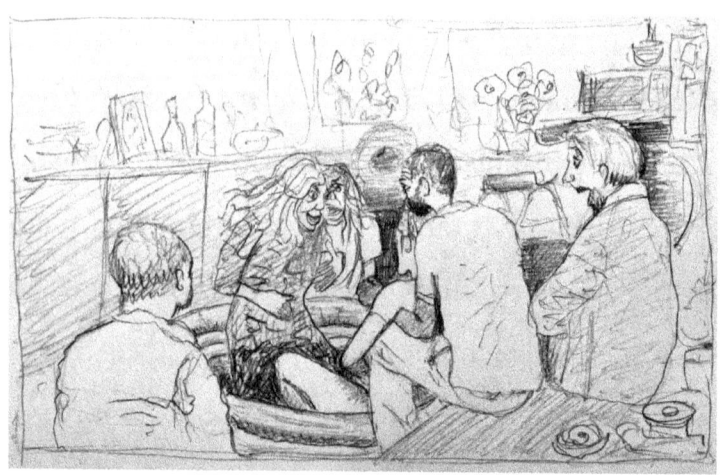

Figure 10 – Rachel Bride Ashton - Pencil drawing impression of Grace and Frankie – *The Lockdown* Series 4 Episode 8 (2018).[10]

The supposed indigenous technique of coaxing the baby out with the words 'here baby baby baby' (fig. 10) to the rolling eyes of her family, has racist and colonial overtones. Here again (though this time

---

[10] Original available at:
https://www.netflix.com/watch/80167676?trackId=2002
57859

the birth is straightforward and successful) the birthing mother, who is already a ridiculed character on account of her hypochondria, is peripheral. In keeping with the formulaic labour narrative and despite being at home, she shouts nonsensically and ignorantly for an epidural. She is portrayed as passive, incapable, completely naïve and disconnected from her body. She wears a t-shirt which reads "My Vagina is My Vagina", which in this context seems to ridicule the concept of consent. The t-shirt highlights her deviance, as does the choice of home birth made under the influence of the deviant mother-in-law (Allemang's counterculture midwife again). The real narrative and comedy come partly from the panicking men, but principally from the last-minute entrance of the ludicrous 'midwife' and her 'dippy' and childlike delight at doing nothing other than catch the baby.

What could have been a woman-empowered birth narrative, while still retaining comedy value, was instead framed as a joke at the expense of both women (The Lockdown, 2018).

Fletcher and Bourgeois assert that in Canada, 'Indigenous birth knowledge, practices and midwives were dismissed as primitive, uneducated, and unsafe' (2015, p.160) and it seems this colonial thinking endures in modern midwife tropes today. These kinds of narratives carelessly dismiss the concept of the dogmatic, controlling institution, instead pointing the finger of patriarchal oppression at the imperious and misguided ideology of natural birth. There are two notable exceptions to the narratives just described. They are the romantic and sentimental waterbirths in the American Soap Opera *The Bold and the Beautiful* – Ridge & Caroline's (2016) and Steffy & Finn's (episode aired on 1 July 2021). Both are peaceful and empowered with the focus on the heterosexual love between the couple and the midwives are unremarkable and peripheral characters. Another less obvious exception is the film, *Pieces of a Woman.* Though the home birth scene could be described as empowered, the mother is ultimately punished by the death of her baby and the midwife is charged with negligence, though later acquitted, creating mixed messages (2020).

Rachel Bride Ashton

Chapter Four

The Sexuality of Birth, Censorship and Visibility without Defiance

I n this chapter I focus on the cultural discomfort we have with acknowledging the sexuality of birth and how this may be behind the censorship of particularly birth-related art, but also vaginal birth in general.

Empowered Birth Paintings

'Is there any subject as unpopular and uncommercial in contemporary art as birth?'
(Jansen, 2019)

Clements describes struggling to find to find birth-related paintings anywhere in the recorded history of art. This massive physical and psychological event which has the potential to happen to approximately half the people in the world, was relegated to the status of a mere 'woman's issue' (Clements, 2019) and therefore not worthy of being recorded in the annals of history. It is, of course, quite possible that birth has been painted down the centuries but just not considered worthwhile or relevant art. There is a wealth of indigenous birth art, but it seems to be not considered worthy of the art world either (Fletcher and Bourgeois, 2015, p153).

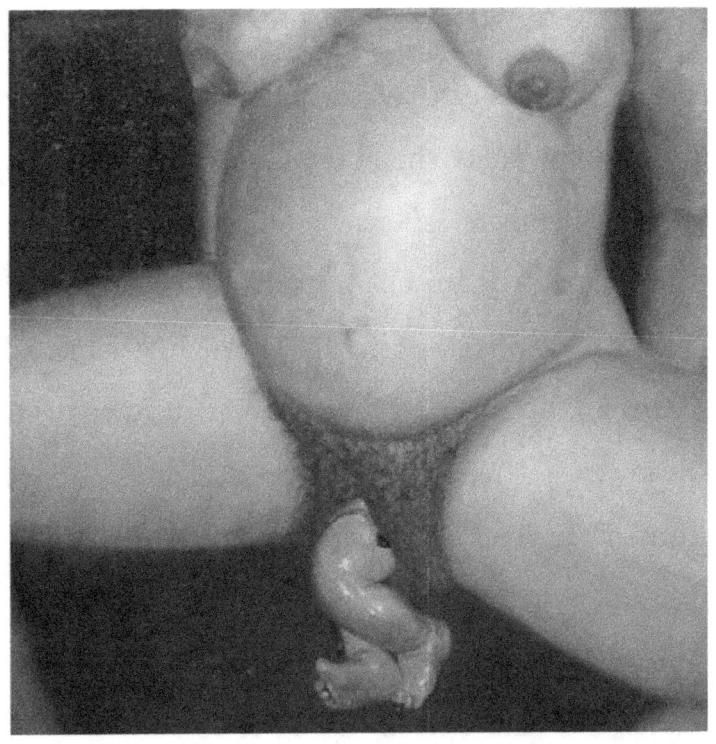

Figure 11 – Jessica Clements – Charity and Izaiah (1997)[11]

---

[11] Available at:
https://citeseerx.ist.psu.edu/viewdoc/download?doi
=10.1.1.460.1212&rep=rep1&type=pdf

Clements' painting, (fig. 11) *Charity and Izaiah* (1997) caused controversy when she tried to display it at the university she attended in Virginia, USA. Several members of staff complained 'that the painting made them uncomfortable', arguing 'that birth is a private affair'. Through Clements' research I discovered a handful of artists who paint empowering birth or raise questions about women's feelings of powerlessness and the lack of medical consent in childbirth – Sara Star, Birgit Amadori, Ghislaine Howard, Jonathan Waller and Jessica Clements herself (fig. 12 & 13).

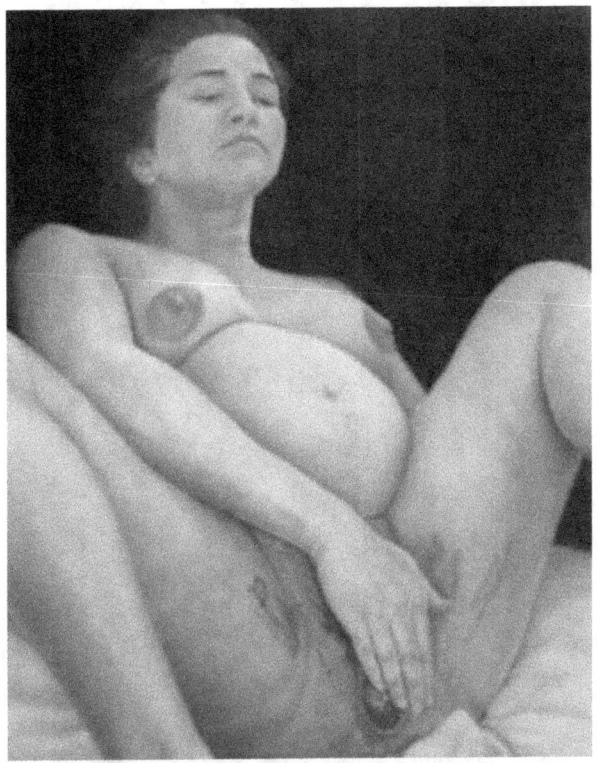

Figure 12 - Jessica Clements - *Heather and Daisy* (2009)[12]

---

[12] Available at:
https://citeseerx.ist.psu.edu/viewdoc/download?doi=10.1.1.460.1212&rep=rep1&type=pdf

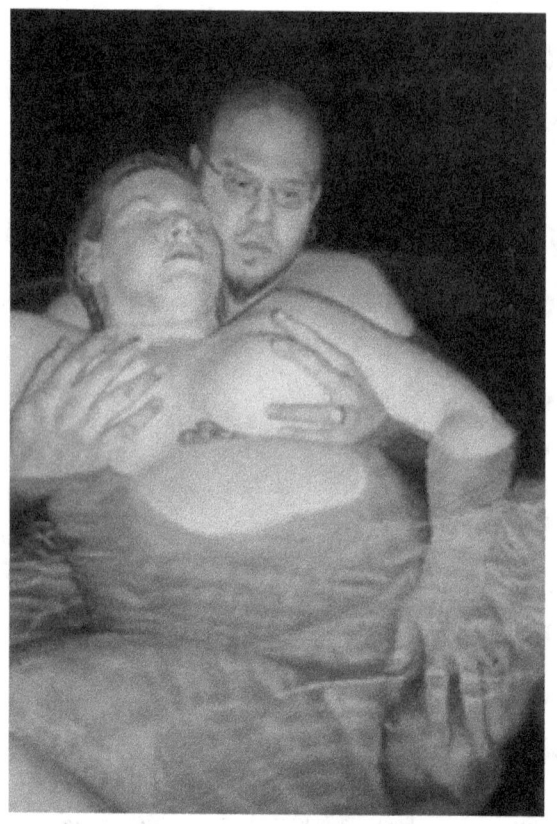

Figure 13 – Jessica Clements - *Jill, Rene, and Sevilen* (2009)[13]

---

[13] Available at:
https://citeseerx.ist.psu.edu/viewdoc/download?doi=10.1.1.460.1212&rep=rep1&type=pdf

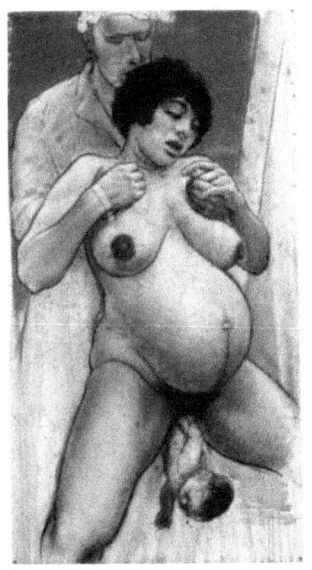 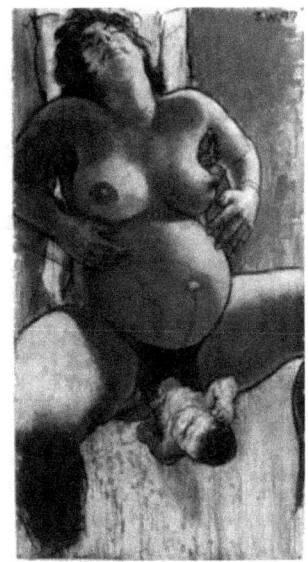

Figure 14 and Figure 15 – Jonathan Waller -
Mother No. 43 and Mother No. 44 (1997)[14]

Jonathan Waller (fig. 14 & 15) paints pictures of predominantly nude birthing women often in supported standing squats.

---

[14] Available at:
https://citeseerx.ist.psu.edu/viewdoc/download?doi=10.1.1.460.1212&rep=rep1&type=pdf

The London gallery who represented Waller prior to 1998 refused to hang his work and ceased to represent him when he began painting his birth series. He has been accused of romanticising and eroticising birth. He admits he may be doing the former but that he sees the work as sensual rather than erotic or titillating (Waller, 2011). He now has work in *The Birth Rites Collection*.

The Birth Rites Collection and Orgasmic Birth

Helen Knowles started *The Birth Rites Collection*, which is currently the only birth dedicated contemporary art collection in the UK. She believes there is no shortage of artists making art about birth, but that they lack places to show the work. Knowles believes that despite it being acceptable for artists to make work about other fundamentally important human subjects, like death, illness, love and sex, birth still seems to remain, overall, taboo. Since its conception in 2006, the collection has faced repeated censorship. Knowles herself has faced censorship for her work and as she tries to install the work in an educational context, is particularly surprised by the reticence of the medical community in these locations (Jansen, 2019).

The collection houses an impressive and divergent selection of art from many artists and includes work by Judy Chicago and Ana Casa Broda (fig. 16). Broda's work 'Kinderwunsch' had ten images from the series removed from public view by Salford University, where they were donated to the collection in 2014.

91

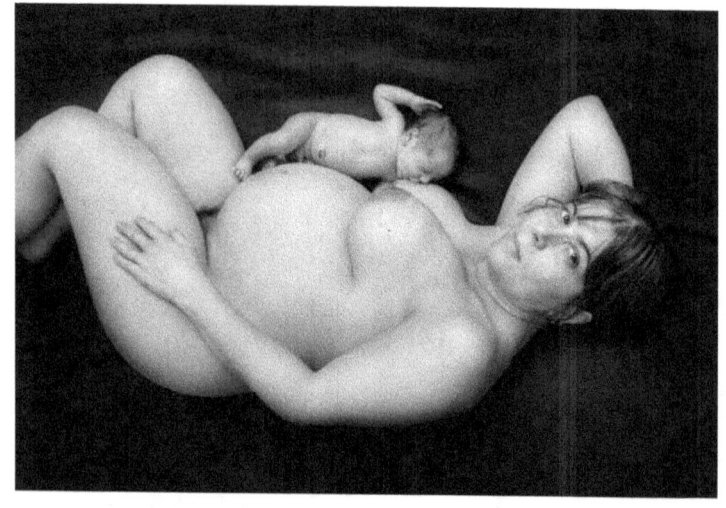

Figure 16 – Anna Casa Broda – *Three Days After Giving Birth to Lucio* (2006 – 12)[15]

An image appropriated from Ina May Gaskins book *A Guide to Childbirth*, by Hermione Wiltshire causes continuing controversy. The

---

[15] Available at:
https://www.birthritescollection.org.uk/the-collection-1/ana-casas-broda

photograph, *Terese in Ecstatic Childbirth* (fig. 17), which I see as an overwhelmingly positive image, caused uproar, when Knowles originally tried to hang it in the entrance to the Science Centre in Glasgow. Knowles couldn't understand why the staff refused to hang it and declined to explain why they felt the need to protect people from an image of a woman in a state of joy, while she gives birth (Jansen, 2019).

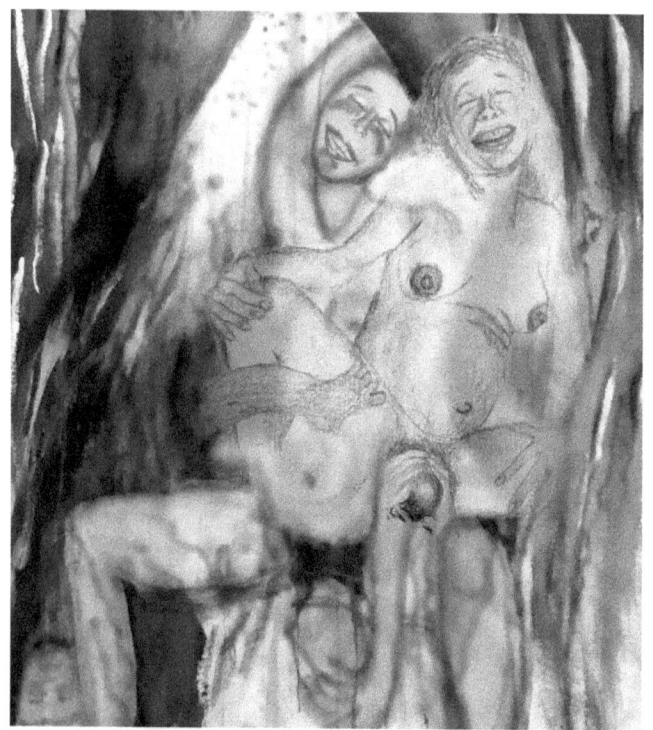

Figure 17 – Rachel Bride Ashton – Mixed Media Collage (2022) after Hermione Wiltshire - *Terese in Ecstatic Childbirth* (2008)[16]

---

[16] Available at:
https://www.birthritescollection.org.uk/the-collection-1/hermione-wiltshire

Knowles herself makes work which includes large, pixelated screen-printed images of stills from found footage of free-birthing women often experiencing sexual pleasure during birth (fig. 18 & 19). She's interested in the tabloid quality these blown-up images evoke and in the ideas of eroticism and obscenity that birth images can elicit and in the fact that this huge bank of birthing imagery exists alongside the multi-million-dollar porn industry's bank of images.

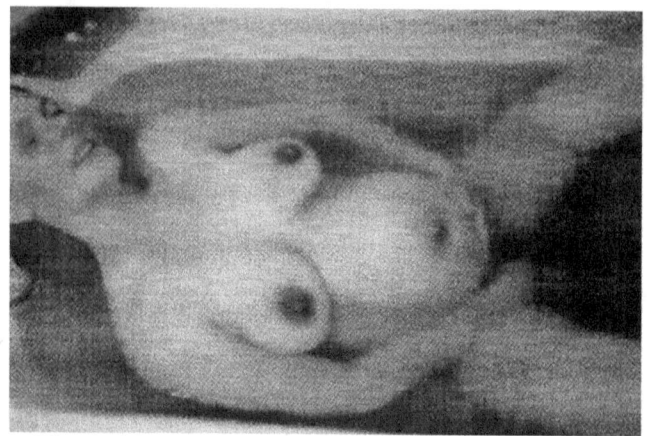

Figure 18 - Helen Knowles - *Birth with orgasm II* (2012)[17]

The suggestion that birth is on the sexual spectrum evidenced by the release of hormones like oxytocin connecting birth, sex, orgasm, breastfeeding and 'skin-to-skin contact with a newborn' (Chawla, 2016) seems to be an area we are very reluctant to discuss or acknowledge. '[Oxytocin was literally

---

[17] Available at: https://www.helenknowles.com

named after the Greek term for "swift Birth'] (Chawla, 2016). Kitzinger believes that a 'Woman's sexuality is perceived as dangerous, and so threatening that its very existence in relation to childbirth may be vigorously denied' (Kitzinger, 1992). Many women have reported that masturbation helps ease the pain of contractions and can speed up a sluggish labour and that sex and masturbation can help kick start labour in the case of women who are overdue, but from my research, this is never shown and seldom, if ever, referenced, in onscreen birth.

Zalka Drglin in *Female Sexuality and Medicine – Sexualisation of Everyday Life, Desexualisation of Childbirth* (2015), believes it is a case of Institutions trying to regulate female sexuality. Sarika Chawla offers, in *The Argument for Masturbating During Childbirth* (2016), that the picture we are given about birth is that it is 'painful and humiliating' and if we were to instead validate the connection between sex and birth, we would see that there is 'no space for sexuality in the delivery room' (Chawla, 2016). If we compare the conditions under which we usually have sex and give birth, it's immediately apparent that they are at opposite ends of the spectrum. Ideally the conditions we would want for both would be the same; 'intimacy, a relaxed environment and the knowledge we are not under anyone's control, ...privacy, a warm, darkened space, [and] no control or comments on [our] appearance or behaviour' (Drglin, 2015).

These conditions are generally easy to facilitate in a home environment and in small midwife units but not so easy in large busy hospitals. Five years ago, the first maternity clinic catering specifically for the needs of people who have a history of sexual abuse, opened. It is now being recognised that not only can women without this kind of history suffer from PTSD as a result of a medically controlled birth (Kitzinger, 2012), but that the ordinary procedures administered during a typical hospital birth can often re-trigger PTSD stemming from past abuse (McCamley, 2016).

Unassisted Birth on YouTube

From my own research on YouTube, I was initially left with the impression that this was a new and hopeful space, a platform capable of allowing a more democratic presentation of birth, a place for visibility without deviance. Woman were posting their positive home birth experiences, videos where they gave birth assisted or unassisted and then had full editing authority over how to present these videos. I found the freebirthing videos initially through Helen Knowles' work, but then realised these were a tiny minority of the kind of births being represented. On further research I read Robyn Longhurst's article *YouTube – A New Space for Birth,* in which Longhurst concluded that videos of natural vaginal birth were more likely to be censored than videos of surgical birth (2009). YouTube, like prime-time TV and cinema, was being curated as a space which is perpetuating and reinforcing cultural beliefs about the medical and surgical models of birth being more acceptable than biological and social models.

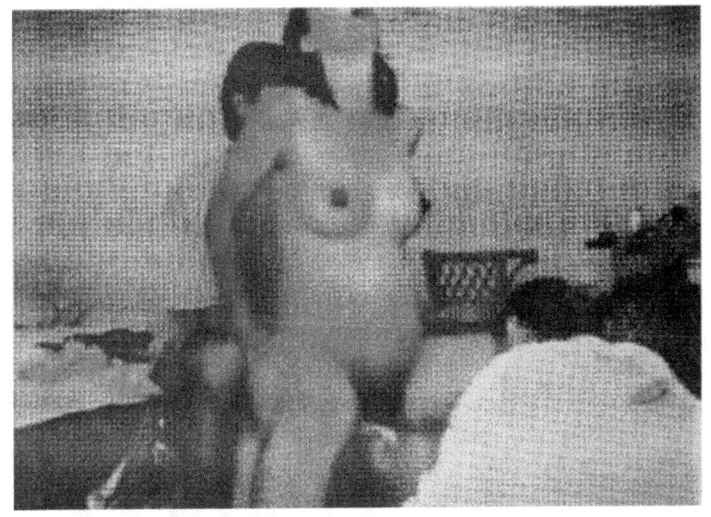

Figure 19 – Helen Knowles - *The Natural Way of Birth* (2012)[18]

Some of the video links Knowles had used as source material, included alongside her work on her website, led to videos which have since been

---

[18] Available at:
https://www.helenknowles.com/index.php/work/youtube_series

censored or removed. Particularly the ones which had some sort of sexual reference in the title, for example *Birth with Orgasm I* or the ones in which there was nudity (fig. 18 & 19). Was YouTube censoring any birth which looked like it had an element of pleasure involved? Again, the sexuality-birth connection seemed to be deemed unacceptable but cutting women open was not. Then I experienced this censorship first hand, when I received an email from YouTube, informing me that a piece of work I had made featuring a natural birth, had been age restricted.

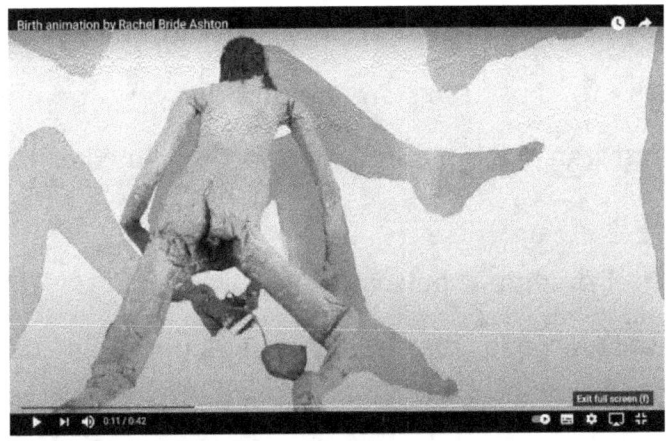

Figure 20 – Rachel Bride Ashton – *Birth Animation* (2020)[19]

The short animation shows a nude paper mâché doll, floating in mid air, giving birth non-violently to instrumental electronic music (fig. 20). While searching for other birth videos, I found no age restrictions on a medical teaching simulation of a

---

[19] Available at:
https://www.youtube.com/watch?v=eFYH5FZTge4

baby being pulled out of a plastic vulva by its head with forceps nor on numerous very graphic Caesarean section surgeries and other medicalised births.

Longhurst believed twelve years ago that YouTube had the potential to 'open up new windows on birth' but that at that point in time it was merely reiterating old discourses (Longhurst, 2009).

Kitzinger said in 2012 that 'traditional birth ways should not be romanticised' and mused that few women would want to give birth in a mud hut far from medical care in case it was needed, but the number of women willing to risk birth alone is growing. Unassisted birth or freebirth is appealing to more women and there is a wealth of online information and radical discussion groups to be found. The Covid-19 pandemic has also contributed to this rise, with the suspension of home births by many NHS trusts in March 2020 (Romanis & Nelson, 2020). There are more than 52K posts referencing 'freebirth' on Instagram in 2022. Kolina Koltai, a researcher "who studies the social media behaviour of alternative health communities" (Zimbelman, 2020) describes this time as "a new digital Wild, Wild West" (cited in Zimbelman, 2020). Less extreme and more hopeful is Katie Vigos' *Empowered Birth Project* (fig. 23) which currently has 450K plus followers on Instagram (2021) and is raising many of the issues I have discussed.

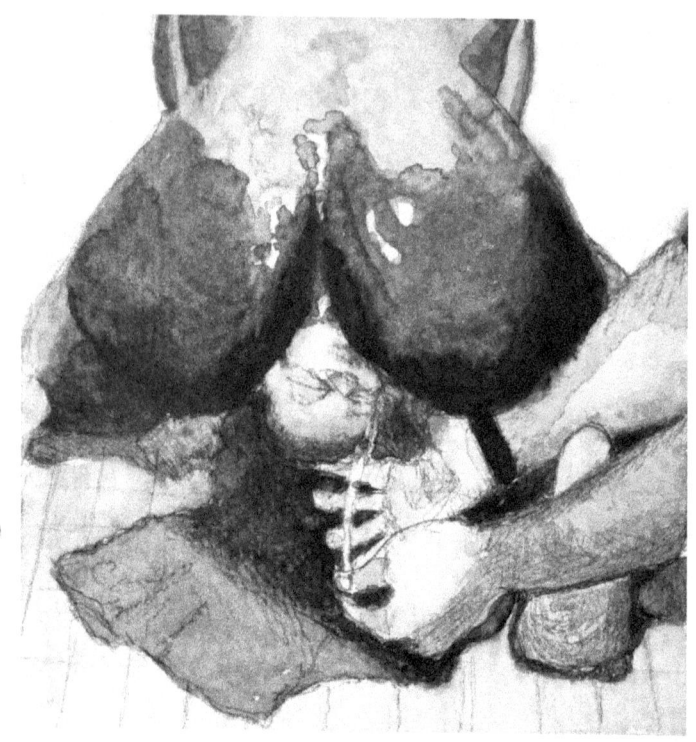

Figure 21 – Rachel Bride Ashton – Watercolour an pencil drawing impression of Vanessa Mendez Photography (2020)[20]

---

[20] Original available at:
https://www.instagram.com/empoweredbirthproject/

Exploring social media more widely, the increased prominence on social media of representations of childbirth in the last decade, which Lauren Bliss says are being afforded 'increasing celebration and dignity' indicate they are no longer considered taboo. She points out that social media has much faster and wider distribution possibilities than cinema, but that both share an 'interest in creating social change through representation.' She concludes 'that any celebration of these images should not overdetermine the effect of representation nor unproblematically subscribe to the belief that visual culture induces measurable change' (Bliss, 2020). However, I would argue that both cinema and social media do have the potential for bringing about change, whether that be considered negative or positive, but that it is certainly difficult to measure. While the capitalist constraints of the mainstream visual media perpetuate the same stagnant birth propaganda, it's clear that the increase in unattended births, for example, has been because of the sharing, availability and accessibility of 'freebirthing' experiences and information on social media.

Conclusion

I began by stating that tropes of invisible and deviant women predominate in the portrayal of birthing women in visual culture today and are used as a form of cultural and social propaganda and I believe I have shown this overwhelmingly to be the case. I have found that whether it be reality- or fiction-based, visual art or media, birthing women are seldom shown with any meaningful voice and personal sovereignty and that positive, female-empowered birth images are continually censored.

While acknowledging that modern obstetrics undoubtedly save lives, the need for special birthing clinics for women who have been sexually abused, and the rise of Freebirthing, suggests that the current system of maternity care is failing women across the board. These real-world invisible women, who feel they have no voice within the system, are instead choosing to absent themselves from it. Rarely are these issues being addressed in Cinema and TV in an un-biased and progressive way. Film and programme makers have a long way to go to in acknowledging the focus on the baby as product, derogatory stereotyping of mothers and systemic medical bias at the heart of these forms of birth entertainment.

Nevertheless, I feel there is some hope that this is beginning to change, with the recent exceptions I mentioned at the end of chapter three and in the art world, which comes with the creation of The Birth Rites collection and in the small but increasing group of artists tackling the issues surrounding birth and its depictions. More art Institutions now need to be willing to represent birth related work. There is also progress in the growing social media space for empowered birth representations and discussion and acknowledgement of obstetric violence. The more artists and advocates for empowered birth find ways to present their work and projects, the more chance there is of a serious dialogue taking place.

There are areas still in need of further investigation, for example, research could be conducted on the link I believe exists between colonialism and the concept of trying to 'eradicate the animal' from birthing women and its effect on reproductive rights worldwide, which I am pursuing in my practical work. Through my interdisciplinary practice, I hope to continually challenge the endorsement of the powerless, invisible, and mute birthing woman: to question our cultural portrayal of ancient, indigenous and modern autonomous birthing choices as deviant and negatively animalistic; to show that in the process of 'civilising' we have 'de-animalised'; and to acknowledge, investigate, expose and nurture our animality, with humour and humility.

References

Allemang, E. (2015) 'Heros and Villains - Representations of Midwives in Ontario's Late Twentieth Century Midwifery Revival' in Burton, N. (ed.) *Natal Signs: Cultural Representations of Pregnancy, Birth and Parenting.* Ontario, Demeter Press, p94-126.

Bear, J. (2006) 'Britney Spears Responds to Daniel Edwards's Sculpture Monument to Pro-Life: The Birth of Sean Preston'. McSweeney's. Available at: https://www.mcsweeneys.net/articles/britney-spears-responds-to-daniel-edwardss-sculpture-monument-to-pro-life-the-birth-of-sean-preston (Accessed 8 January 2022).

Berger, J. (1972) *Ways of Seeing.* London: Penguin Books.

Birth Rites Collection (2017) [Exhibition] King's College, London. 2017- present.

Bliss, L. (2020) 'What Are You Expecting to See? On Childbirth in Visual Culture'. *Research Gate.* Available at: https://www.researchgate.net/publication/3441052 85_What_Are_You_Expecting_to_See_On_Childbi rth_in_Visual_Culture (Accessed 9 June 2021).

Block, J. (2007) *Pushed: The Painful Truth About Childbirth and Modern Maternity Care.* USA. Da Capo Press.

Bohren, M. (2019) 'How Women are Treated During Facility-Based Childbirth in Four Countries: A Cross-Sectional Study with Labour Observations and Community-Based Surveys'. *The Lancet*. Available at: https://www.thelancet.com/journals/lancet/article/PIIS0140-6736(19)31992-0/fulltext (Accessed 8 July 2021).

Bourgeois, C. & Fletcher, C. (2015) 'Refusing Delinquency, Reclaiming Power – Indigenous Woman and Childbirth', in Burton, N. (ed.) *Natal Signs: Cultural Representations of Pregnancy, Birth and Parenting*. Ontario, Demeter Press, p153-171.

Chawla, S. (2016) 'The Argument for Masturbating During Childbirth'. *Vice*. Available at: https://www.vice.com/en/article/jma3zb/the-argument-for-masturbating-during-childbirth (Accessed 15 June 2021).

Clements, J. (2009) *The Origin of the World: Women's Bodies and Agency in Childbirth*. MA Thesis. George Mason University. Available at: https://citeseerx.ist.psu.edu/viewdoc/download?doi=10.1.1.460.1212&rep=rep1&type=pdf (Accessed 3 May 2021).

Clugston, H. (2018) 'Damien Hirst's gigantic uteruses are a bold correction to shocking ignorance', *The Guardian*, 19 November. Available at: https://www.theguardian.com/artanddesign/2018/nov/19/damien-hirst-uterus-sculptures-qatar-sidra-medicine-hospital (Accessed 20 April 2021).

Collen, A. (2015) *10% Human – How Your Body's Microbes Hold the Key to Health and Happiness.* London: William Collins.

Drglin, Z. (2015) *Female Sexuality and Medicine – Sexualisation of Everyday Life, Desexualisation of Childbirth.* London: IntechOpen. Available at: DOI: 10.5772/60124. (Accessed 1 June 2021).

Dundes, L. (1987) 'The Evolution of Maternal Birthing Position'. Vol. 77 (AJPH May, No. 5.) *Public Health Then and Now.* Available at: https://ajph.aphapublications.org/doi/pdf/10.2105/AJPH.77.5.636. (Accessed 9 July 2021).

Einion, A. (2015) 'Resistance and Submission – A Critique of Representations of Birth', in Burton, N. (ed.) *Natal Signs: Cultural Representations of Pregnancy, Birth and Parenting.* Ontario, Demeter Press, p172-193.

'Episode 117' (2016) *The Bold and the Beautiful,* Season 29, CBS, 7 March 2016.

'Episode 76' (2021) *The Bold and the Beautiful,* Season 34, CBS, 1 July 2021.

'Episode 7' (2021) *Sex Education.* Season 3. Eleven. Available at: Netflix (Accessed 8 January 2022).

Figes, L. (2020) '7 artists who radically changed the way we document pregnancy'. *Dazed.* Available at: https://www.dazeddigital.com/art-photography/article/47432/1/artists-radically-changed-documentations-pregnancy-beyonce-sally-mann-nan-goldin (Accessed 10 July 2021).

'Firstborn for Internet Dating Soulmates' (2014) *Newborn Russia*, Season 2, episode 23. RT Documentary Channel, 22 April.

Hutton, E. et al (2020) 'Perinatal or Neonatal Mortality Among Women who Intend at the Onset of Labour to Give Birth at Home Compared to Women of Low Obstetrical Risk Who Intend to Give Birth in Hospital: A Systematic Review and Meta-Analysis.' *The Hub*. Available at: https://www.pslhub.org/learn/patient-safety-in-health-and-care/high-risk-areas/maternity/perinatal-or-neonatal-mortality-among-women-who-intend-at-the-onset-of-labour-to-give-birth-at-home-compared-to-women-of-low-obstetrical-risk-who-intend-to-give-birth-in-hospital-a-systematic-review-and-meta-analyses-r2646/ (Accessed 9 July 2021).

Jansen, C. (2019) 'Birth Rites: The Only Collection of Contemporary Art on Childbirth.' *Elephant*. Available at: https://elephant.art/birth-rites-collection-contemporary-art-childbirth/ (Accessed 8 July 2021).

Jolly, N. (2015) 'Does Labour Mean Work? A Look at the Meaning of Birth in Amish and Non-Amish Society', in Burton, N. (ed.) *Natal Signs: Cultural Representations of Pregnancy, Birth and Parenting*. Ontario, Demeter Press, p218-231.

Karremann, I. (2004) 'I'd Rather Be a Cyborg than a Goddess': Reading the Cyborg Poetics of Eavan Boland'. *JSTOR*. Nordic Irish Studies, vol. 3 (pp. 113–126). Available at: www.jstor.org/stable/30001509 (Accessed 28 August 2021).

Kasprzak, E. (2019) 'Why are Black Mothers More at Risk of Dying?' *BBC News*. Available at: https://www.bbc.co.uk/news/uk-england-47115305 (Accessed 29 January 2021).

Kitzinger, S. (1992) *Ourselves as Mothers*. London: Doubleday.

Kitzinger, S. (2012) 'Rediscovering the Social Model of Childbirth', Birth Issues in Perinatal Care'. *Wiley Online Libra*ry. Volume 39 (Issue 4) Available at: https://doi-org.libezproxy.dundee.ac.uk/10.1111/birt.12005 (Accessed 12 August 2021).

Limb, M. (2021) 'Disparity in maternal deaths because of ethnicity is "unacceptable"'. *The BMJ*. Available at: https://doi.org/10.1136/bmj.n152 (Accessed 27 August 2021).

Longhurst, R. (2009) 'Youtube: A New Space for Birth?' Feminist Review. *Sage Journals*. Available at: https://doi.org/10.1057%2Ffr.2009.22 (Accessed 30 August 2021).

McCamley, F. (2016) 'UK's first maternity clinic for rape victims opens'. *BBC*. Available at: https://www.bbc.co.uk/news/uk-36917746 (Accessed 2 June 2021).

Nall, J. (2011) *Interrogating Social Conceptualizations of Childbirth and Gender, an Ecofeminist Analysis*. PhD Thesis. Florida Atlantic University. Available at: https://fau.digital.flvc.org/islandora/object/fau%3A3798/datastream/OBJ/view/Interrogating_social_conceptualizations_of_childbirth_and_gender.pdf (Accessed 5 August 2021).

Newborn Russia (2014) RT Documentary Channel, 26 March.

Newnham, E. et al (2017) 'Paradox of the Institution: Findings from a Hospital Labour Ward Ethnography'. *BMC Pregnancy and Childbirth.* Available at: https://bmcpregnancychildbirth.biomedcentral.com /articles/10.1186/s12884-016-1193-4 (Accessed 8 July 2021).

Noble, E & Keenan, L (2021) 'Caesarean Section Rates Continue to Rise, Amid Growing Inequalities in Access'. *World Health Organisation.* Available at: https://www.who.int/news/item/16-06-2021- caesarean-section-rates-continue-to-rise-amid- growing-inequalities-in-access-who (Accessed 28 Aug 2021).

Nonacs, R. (2020) 'Childbirth-Related PTSD and Postpartum Depression Commonly Occur Together'. *MGH Centre.* Available at: https://womensmentalhealth.org/posts/childbirth- related-ptsd/ (Accessed 29 Aug 2021).

Petchesky, R.P. (1987) 'Fetal Images: The Power of Visual Culture in the Politics of Reproduction'. *Jstor.* Available at: https://www.jstor.org/stable/3177802?seq=6#meta data_info_tab_contents (Accessed 20 June 2021).

Phillips, S. (2018) '8 Facts About Epidural Side Effects'. *Parents.* Available at: https://www.parents.com/pregnancy/giving- birth/epidural/epidural-side-effects/ (Accessed 7th January 2022).

Pieces of a Woman (2020) Directed by Kornél Mundruczó. Available at: Netflix (Accessed 1 March 2021).

Rink, L. (2012) *"Even More Scared": The Effects of Childbirth Reality Shows on Young Women's Perceptions of Birth.* BA Honors Thesis. University of Michigan. Available at: https://deepblue.lib.umich.edu/bitstream/handle/2027.42/91860/lrink.pdf?sequence=1 (Accessed 13 July 2021).

Romanis, E. & Nelson, A. (2020) 'Homebirthing in the United Kingdom during COVID-19'. *Sage Journals.* Available at: https://doi.org/10.1177%2F0968533220955224 (Accessed 11 July 2021).

Savage, M. (2021) 'Britney Spears officially requests new conservator to replace her father'. *BBC.* Available at: https://www.bbc.co.uk/news/entertainment-arts-57982252 (Accessed 28 July 2021).

Stejskalova, T. (2021) 'No creation without destruction: images of childbirth and Candice Breitz's Labour'. *Journal of Visual Art Practice -Taylor & Francis Online.* Vol 20 (Issue 1-2) Available at: https://www.tandfonline.com/doi/full/10.1080/14702029.2021.1917907 (Accessed 10 July 2021).

Sulcas, R. (2020) '500 Years of Pregnant Women in Art'. *New York Times.* Available at: https://www.nytimes.com/2020/03/13/arts/design/pregnant-women-art.html (Accessed 10 July 2021).

Summers, H. (2021) 'Black women are four times more likely to die during pregnancy or childbirth in the UK and America'. *The Guardian.* Available at: https://www.theguardian.com/global-development/2021/jan/15/black-women-in-the-uk-four-times-more-likely-to-die-in-pregnancy-or-childbirth (Accessed 7 July 2021).

Takeshita, C. (2017) 'From Mother/Fetus to Holobiont(s): A Material Feminist Ontology of the Pregnant Body'. *Catalyst Journal.* Available at: https://catalystjournal.org/index.php/catalyst/article/view/28787/html_5 (Accessed 15 July 2021).

The Birth Reborn (2013) Directed by E. Chauvet. Available at: Netflix (Accessed 23 July 2021).

'The Lockdown' (2018) *Grace and Frankie.* Season 4 Episode 8. Okay Goodnight; Skydance Television. Available at: Netfilx (Accessed: 20 June 2021).

Waller, J. (2011) *Birth as Confrontational Image.* [Podcast] Birth Rites Collection. Available at: https://static1.squarespace.com/static/60362110a2966e5868f158cd/t/60423636a32c6111c202fbc0/1623400847250/Birth+as+Confrontational+Image.mp3/original/Birth+as+Confrontational+Image.mp3 (Accessed 25 June 2021).

Watkins, A. (2019) 'Birthing Positions: Supporting a Woman's Choice in Labour'. *Ausmed.* Available at: https://www.ausmed.co.uk/cpd/articles/birthing-positions (Accessed 20 June 2021).

Williams, S. (1994) Review of *Motherhood and Representation: The Mother in Popular Culture and Melodrama* by E. Ann Kaplan. JSTOR. Available at: https://doi.org/10.2307/3340736 (Accessed 21 June 2021).

Zimbelman, A. (2020) 'I Brainwashed Myself with the Internet'. *NBC News.* Available at:

https://www.nbcnews.com/news/us-news/she-wanted-freebirth-no-doctors-online-groups-convinced-her-it-n1140096 (Accessed 19 July 2021).

Rachel Bride Ashton

Bibliography

Bynum, B. (2008) 'The McKeown Thesis'. *The Lancet.* Available at: https://www.thelancet.com/journals/lancet/article/PIIS0140673608602925/fulltext (Accessed 20 February 2021).

Cahill, H.A. (2001) 'Male appropriation and medicalization of childbirth: an historical analysis'. *Journal of Advanced Nursing.* Available at: https://onlinelibrary.wiley.com/doi/full/10.1046/j.1365-2648.2001.01669.x?saml_referrer (Accessed 7 February 2021).

Colgrove, J. (2002) 'The McKeown Thesis: A Historical Controversy and Its Enduring Influence'. *American Journal of Public Health.* Available at: https://www.ncbi.nlm.nih.gov/pmc/articles/PMC1447153/ (Accessed 20 February 2021).

Davis-Floyd, R. (2001) 'The Technocratic, Humanistic, and Holistic Paradigms of Childbirth'. *International Journal of Gynecology and Obstetrics* 75, pp. S5–S23. Available at: https://obgyn-onlinelibrary-wiley-com.libezproxy.dundee.ac.uk/doi/full/10.1016/S0020-7292(01)00510-0 (Accessed 2 February 2021).

De Benedictis, S. et al (2019) 'Quantitative insights into televised birth: a content analysis of One Born Every Minute'. *Taylor & Francis Online.* Available at: https://www.tandfonline.com/doi/full/10.1080/15295036.2018.1516046 (Accessed 26 January 2021).

Federici, S. (2004), *Caliban and the Witch – Women, the Body and Primitive Accumulation.* New York, Autonomedia.

Glosswitch (2016) 'Birth Wars: The Politics of Childbirth'. *The New Statesman.* Available at: https://www.newstatesman.com/politics/feminism/2016/05/birth-wars-politics-childbirth (Accessed 7 February 2021).

Haraway, D. (1991) 'A Cyborg Manifesto – Science, Technology and Socialist-Feminism in the Late Twentieth Century' in Bell, D. and Kennedy, B.M. (ed.) *Cybercultures Reader.* London, Routledge, Chapter 18, p298. Available at: https://warwick.ac.uk/fac/arts/english/currentstudents/undergraduate/modules/fulllist/special/transnational/haraway-cyborgmanifesto-1.pdf (Accessed 11 Aug 2021).

Hart, N. (1985) *The Sociology of Health and Medicine.* Ormskirk, Causeway.

Loves Labor Lost, ER. Season 1, Episode 19 (1995) NBC (9 March)

Leachman, C. (2019) 'Most women give birth in hospital – but it's got more to do with World War II than health'. *The Conversation.* Available at: https://theconversation.com/most-women-give-birth-in-hospital-but-its-got-more-to-do-with-world-war-ii-than-health-110647 (Accessed 8 March 2021).

Mulins, J. (2015) 'The 12 Most Memorable Birth Moments in Movies'. *Eonline.* Available at: https://www.eonline.com/uk/news/648399/the-12-most-memorable-birth-moments-in-movies (Accessed 25 January 2021).

Reynolds, D. (2018) Natural Birth: 'The Long Struggle of Dr. Ágnes Geréb'. *The Technoskeptic.* Available at: https://thetechnoskeptic.com/struggle-agnes-gereb/ (Accessed 3 April 2021).

Ritchie, K. & Simonpillai, R. (2021) 'Pieces of A Woman: Midwives on the accuracy of the home birth scene'. *Now.* Available at: https://nowtoronto.com/movies/pieces-of-a-woman-midwives-accuracy-home-birth-scene (Accessed 9 February 2021).

Sailing Away, ER. Season 7, Episode 19 (2001) NBC (25 April)

Scudellari, M. (2017) 'Cleaning up the Hygiene Hypothesis'. *PNAS.* Available at: https://www.ncbi.nlm.nih.gov/pmc/articles/PMC5320962/ (Accessed 6 March 2021).

Sturken, M. & Cartwright, L. (2009) *Practices of Looking - An Introduction to Visual Culture.* New York, Oxford University Press.

Uppal, D. (2014). The art of midwifery: Can creative images of birth enhance holistic care? *Nurse Education in Practice,* 14(3), 311–318. Available at: https://doi.org/10.1016/j.nepr.2014.01.013 (Accessed 25 January).

Winant, C. (2016) 'The Art of Birth'. *Contemporary Art Review*. Available at: https://contemporaryartreview.la/the-art-of-birth/ (Accessed 25 January 2021).

About the Birth Rites Collection

The Birth Rites Collection was founded by curator, Helen Knowles in 2009. This was following a touring exhibition curated by Knowles working alongside Phoebe Mortimer on public programmes. *Birth Rites* commissioned 5 artworks by Hermione Wiltshire, Ping Qiu, Suzanne Holtom, Jaygo Bloom and Andy Lawrence and premiered at the Glasgow Science Centre and Manchester Museum in 2008.

Birth Rites is a collection of contemporary art on childbirth, the first of its kind in the world. It was housed in the Mary Seacole Building in the Midwifery School at the University of Salford from

2009-2017 and King's College, London from 2017 - 2021, across four buildings on Guy's Campus. The collection is currently housed at the University of Kent and comprises photography, sculpture, painting, artist books, print, wallpaper, drawing, new media and film.

The Birth Rites Collection aims to facilitate the production of new cutting edge works by artists who might not normally address the subject because of its taboo status within contemporary art practice, to support the work of artists whose work already engages with issues on this subject and to acquire relevant existing works to expand the collection.

Through the presentation and dissemination of the work in the public domain, the BRC encourages debate and increases awareness around childbirth practice. The project highlights issues such as the shift towards medical intervention in birth and explores the impact of biomedical advances in technology. They explore whether society's focus on propelling women onto an equal footing with men in the workplace, erodes their importance as mothers and investigates how free women are to give birth in a way they want. The Birth Rites Collection considers who controls the process of childbirth and why.

The collection receives donations of artworks to the collection from artists. It occasionally commissions artworks. They have functioned in this way since the beginning and if it was not for the amazing support of all their artists, the collection would not exist. This is a two-way process where they aim to support and promote each and every artist who donates. If you are interested in donating a work, please email the curator. All works are considered from contemporary artists.

https://www.birthritescollection.org.uk

Artist's Statement:

Rachel Bride Ashton

Multi-species interconnectedness, biophilia and feminine intuition come together in an ever-expanding field of film, sound, sculpture and painting. The multi-media installation is woven together with biomorphic tentacles of salvaged waste and borrowed earth materials.

The work is produced through a cyclical, organic, multi-disciplinary creative process whereby research, 2D and 3D installation, performance and film generate characters, scenarios and microcosms.

I challenge our cultural de-animalisation and particularly the institution-controlled birth portrayal dominant in our onscreen culture while celebrating the 90% non-human part of us, our microbiome, formed at birth. In my short films, I play a hairy, animal-woman, celebrating good bacteria and its sources, who, though ridiculous, also embodies a deep melancholic longing for female body autonomy and a more sympathetic connection between the human and non-human.

I have created a vivid, chaotic, Utopian world where the visceral, intuitive beast-woman and her effluvia are raised up, thrust up, into the censored, phobic, Apollonian realm. She is put in a position of worship, like Baubo, the Vulvanic Goddess of Obsenity or an ancient Sheela-Na-Gig. Orgasmic and seeping, she defies our flush-away, sterile, medicated, anthropocentric lifestyles and honours our excretions as rich earth contributions processed by the busy agents of decomposition or *Chthonic Ones.*

Rachel Bride Ashton

.

Author's artwork (2022)

Rachel Bride Ashton

Rachel Bride Ashton

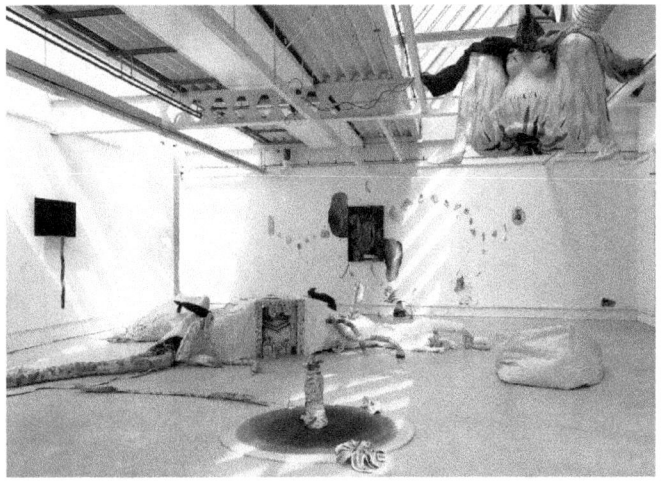

Rachel Bride Ashton

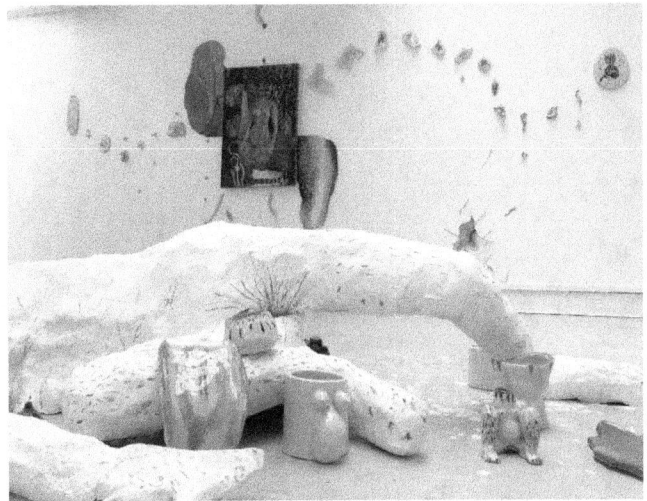

Rachel Bride Ashton

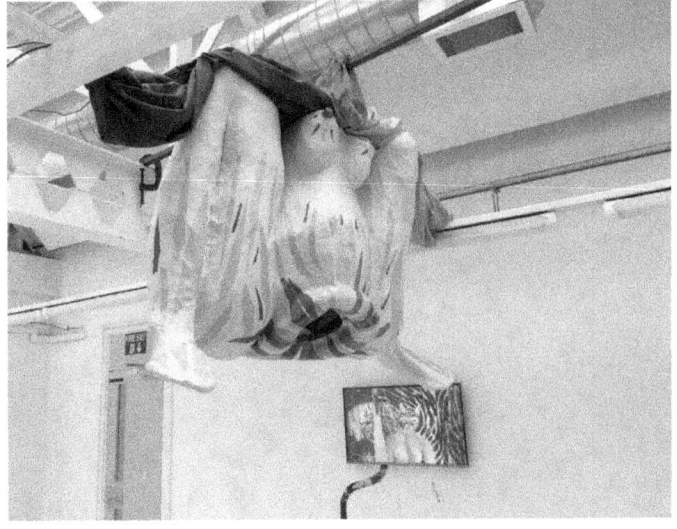

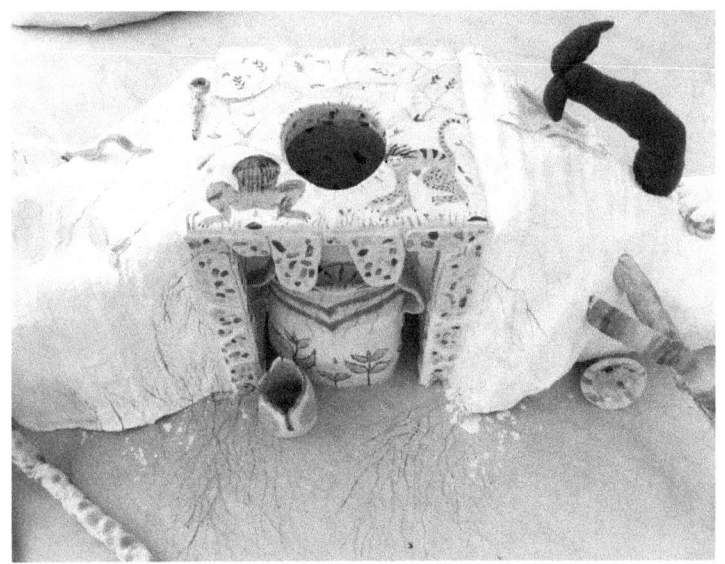

Rachel Bride Ashton

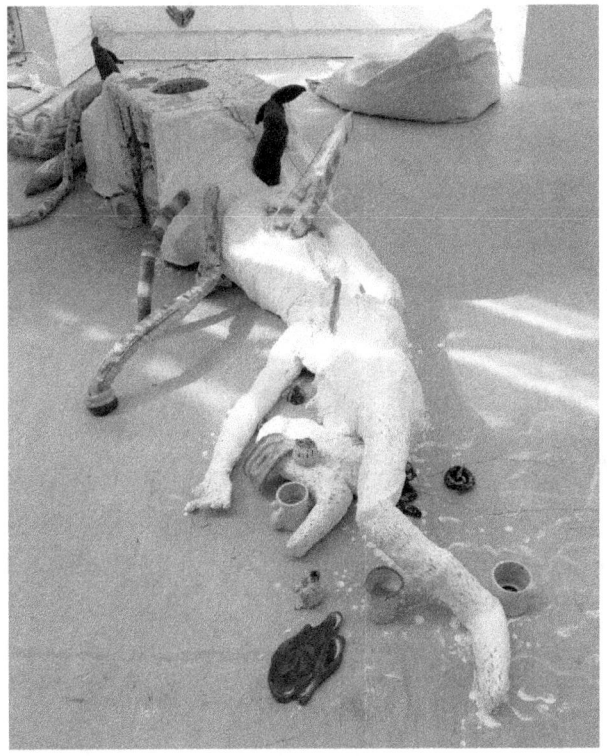

Rachel Bride Ashton

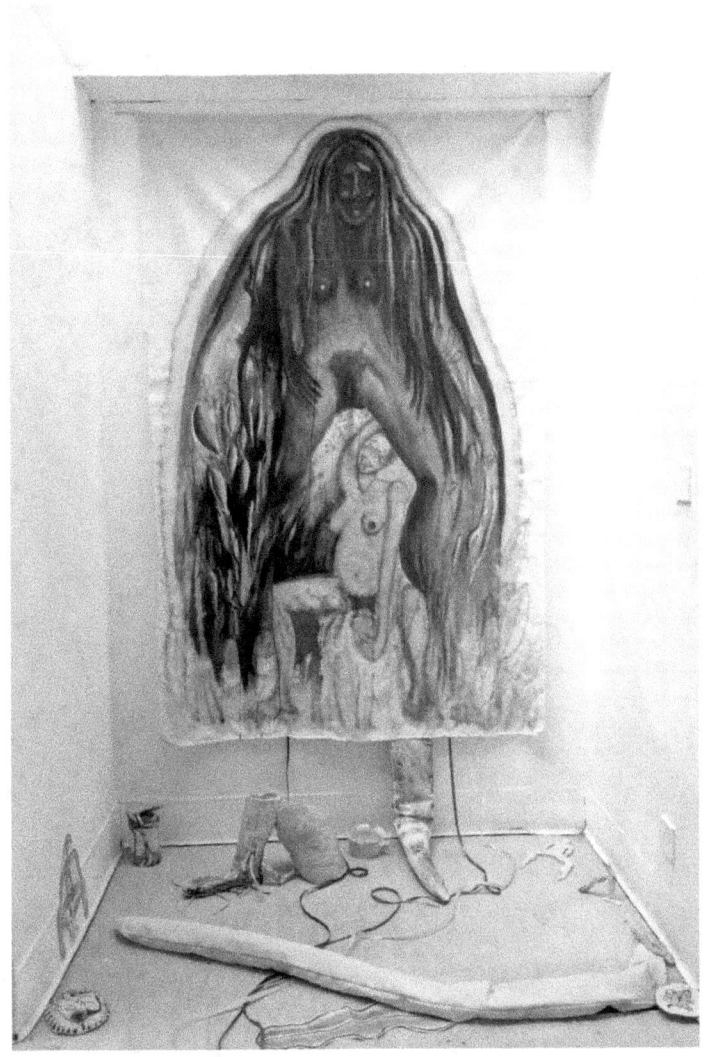

Rachel Bride Ashton

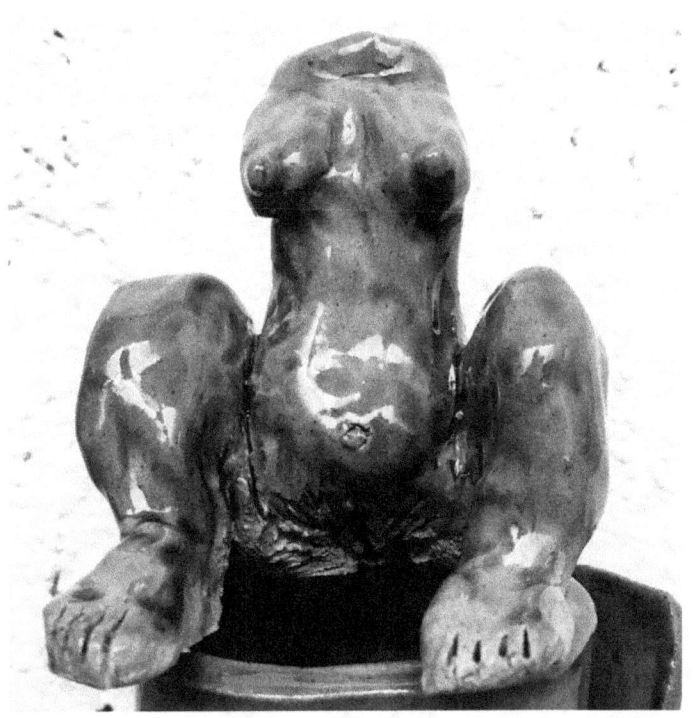

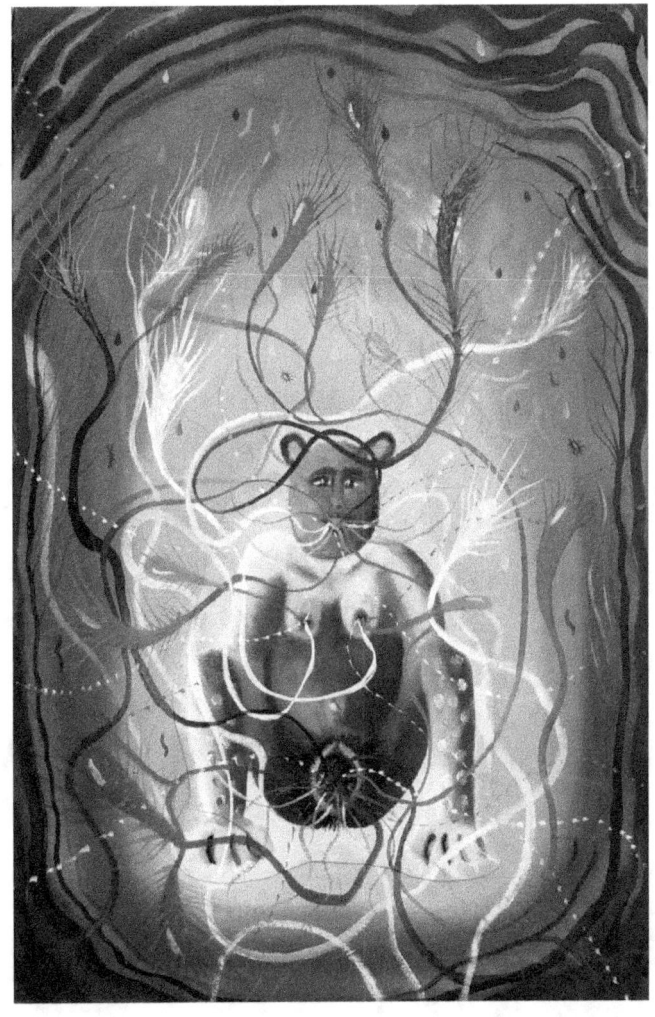

Rachel Bride Ashton

Acknowledgements

I would like to thank my sister Anna, for her belief in my academic skills, encouragement and feedback and to my mother and father for this also and for their very thorough and helpful proof readings, despite differing opinions on commas!

Thank you to my daughter Gudrun for her excellent feedback and tips on sentence structure and to both my son, Gwyn and Gudrun for giving me the powerfully unparalleled experiences of two magical homebirths which inspired much of the work and research I have done since.

Thank you to my husband Charlie for always being there and listening to me and telling me how clever I am!

Thank you to all my friends everywhere past and present who have supported me and allowed me to think I am worth listening to and my tutors at DJCAD for their interest and encouragement and to my academic supervisor Anna Notaro and to Helen Gorrill for their support and for being such champions of women in academia and the arts.

BOOM!

This book was originally submitted as a dissertation in partial fulfilment of the requirements of a Bachelor of Arts (Hons) degree in Fine Art at the Duncan of Jordanstone College of Art and Design, the University of Dundee, in 2022.

Rachel Bride Ashton

A note about Boom Graduates

We propel graduates forward so they can make their mark on the world - we push the boundaries, share brilliant ideas and inspire possibility. We publish dissertations as books, presented gift-boxed at graduation ceremonies, delivering brand-new research to the world quicker than anyone else. We plant trees for every commissioned book sold, and give our Boom graduates the chance to profit-share from their brilliant ideas. Furthermore we donate the majority of our profits to funding research and scholarship for disadvantaged students who wouldn't normally be able to attend university. Through academic excellence and environmental sustainability, *Boom Graduates* are changing the world.

We are Boom Graduates - an imprint of Boom Publications Ltd. We are a more-than-profit company, dedicating over half our profits to providing university scholarships for underprivileged students across the world. We aim to become the globe's biggest provider of such scholarships – and if like Rachel, the author of this book, you'd also like to contribute to making the world a better place, please contact us: we publish monographs, edited books, and moreover our graduate series – Boom Graduates – are presented at graduation days across the world in archival, lined museum-quality presentation cases, engraved with the graduate's name and award.

Boom Publications are based at the Duncan of Jordanstone College of Art and Design, at the University of Dundee in Scotland. We were one of the winners of the 2022 Venture awards hosted by the Centre for Entrepreneurship, and have since been shortlisted for the Converge Challenge, a national award that brings together ambitious and creative thinkers with innovative ideas to work with industry experts to transform their ideas into sustainable companies operating in the commercial world. We are also climate conscious and work with agencies to plant a tree for each and every book commissioned, offsetting thousands of tonnes of carbon each year. Follow us on social media to watch our forest grow @boomgraduates.

Thank you for contributing by purchasing this book. Please visit our catalogues on www.boompublications.com.

Notes

Rachel Bride Ashton

Rachel Bride Ashton

Rachel Bride Ashton

Rachel Bride Ashton